JAPANESE
COLORING BOOK

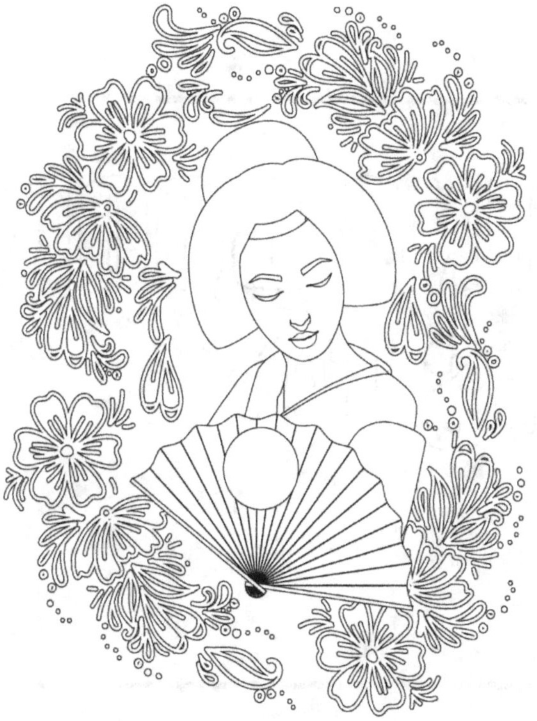

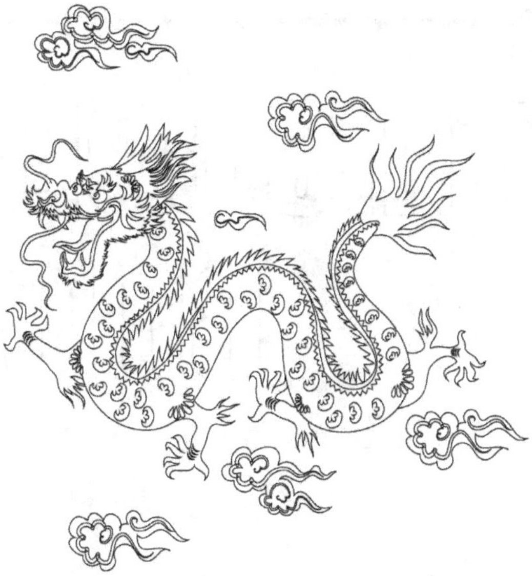

— Sekai Publishing —

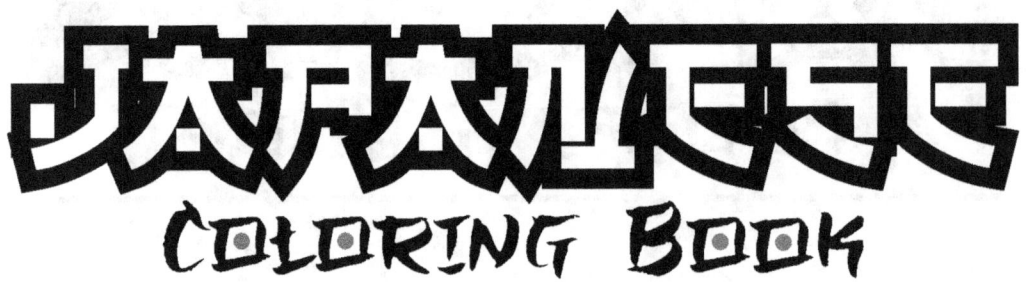

JAPANESE
COLORING BOOK

THIS COLORING BOOK
BELONGS TO

_____

_____

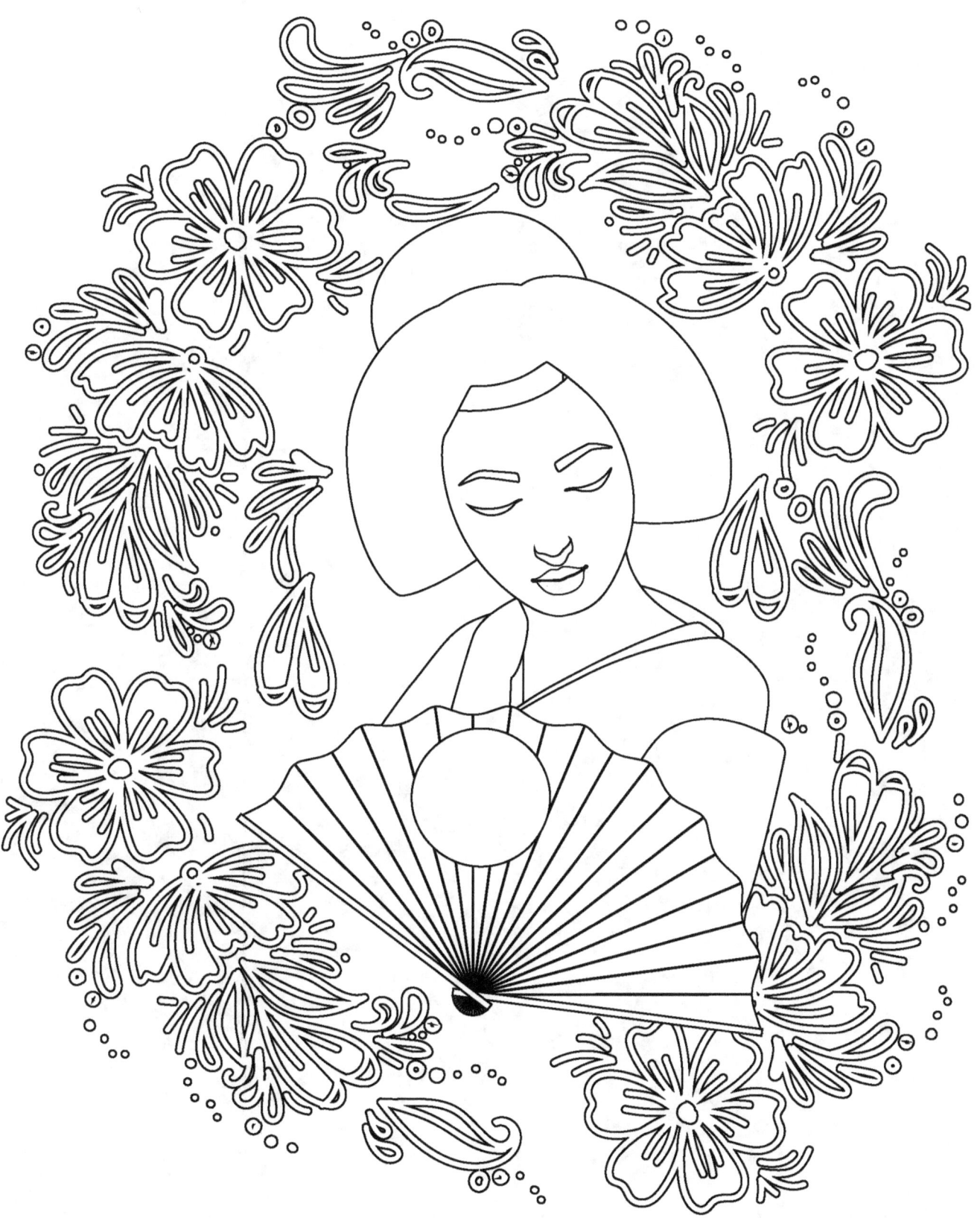

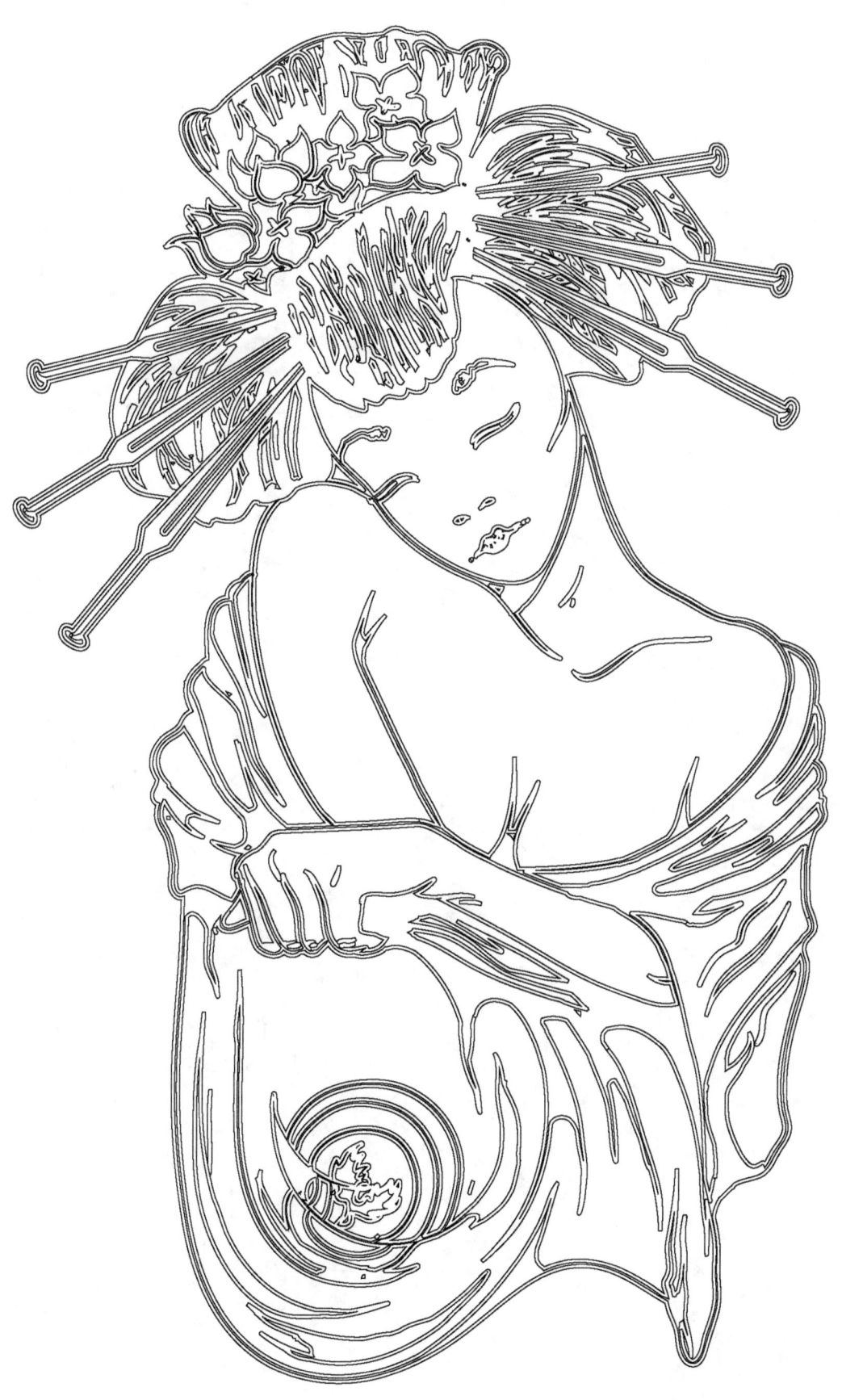

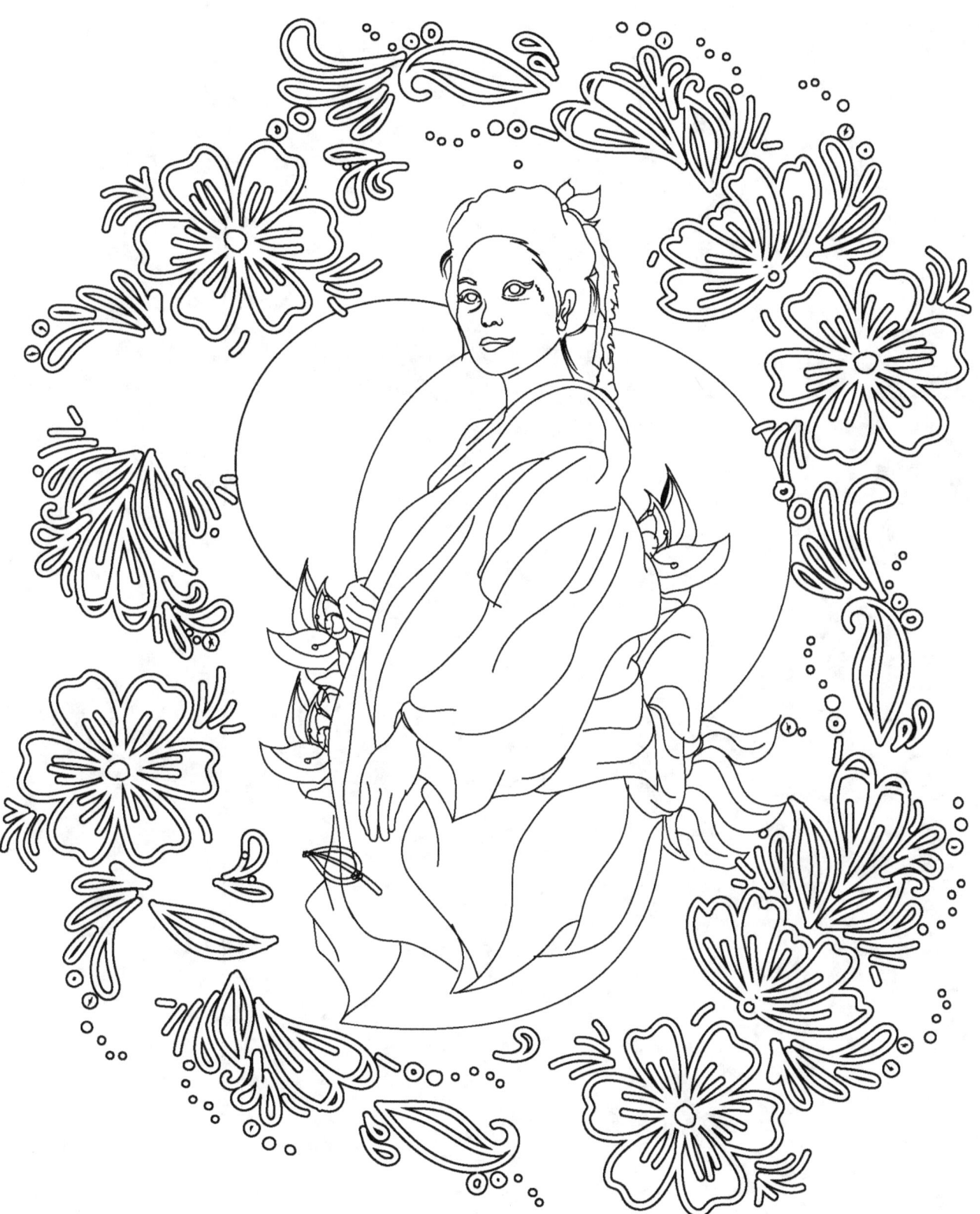

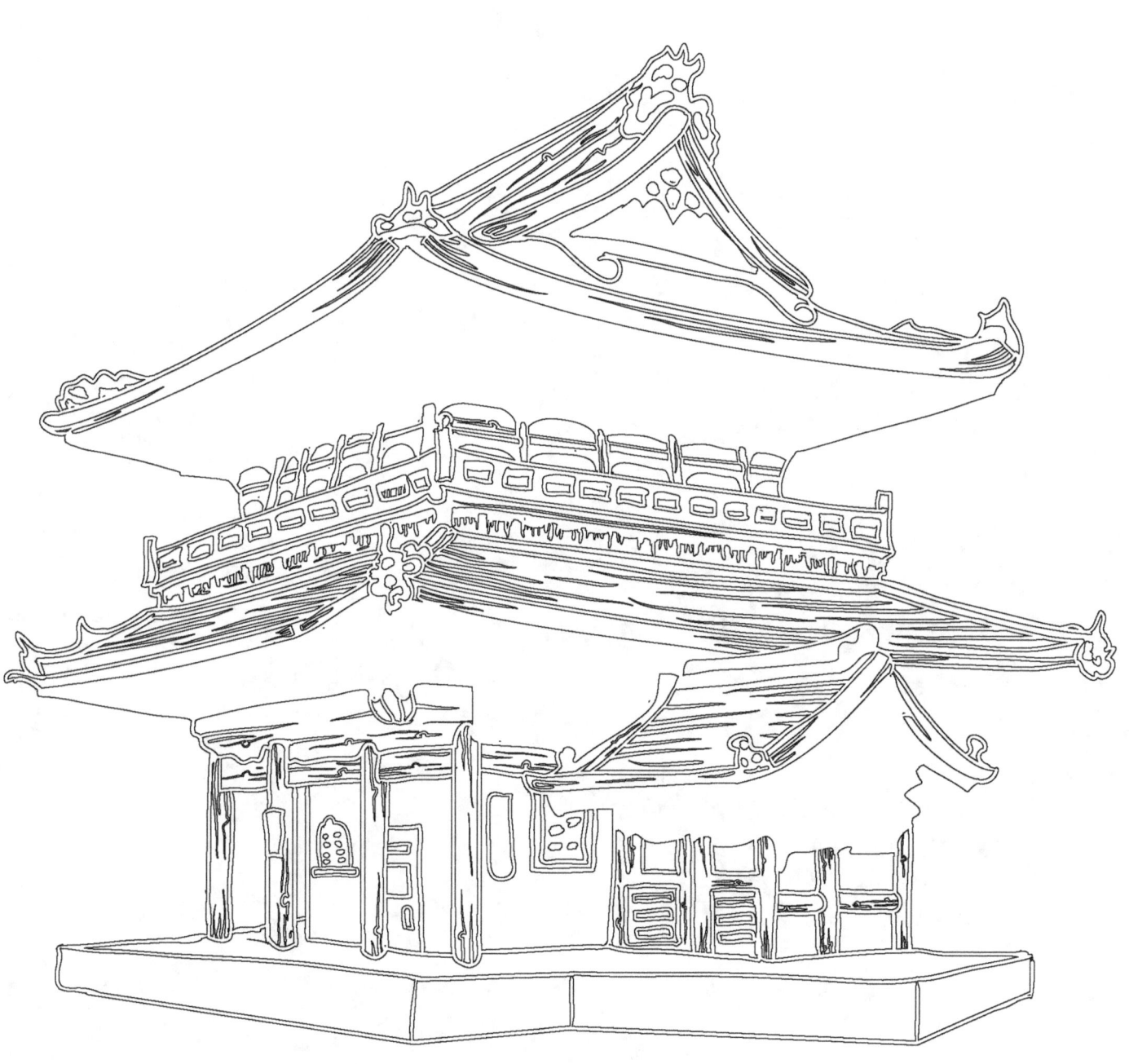

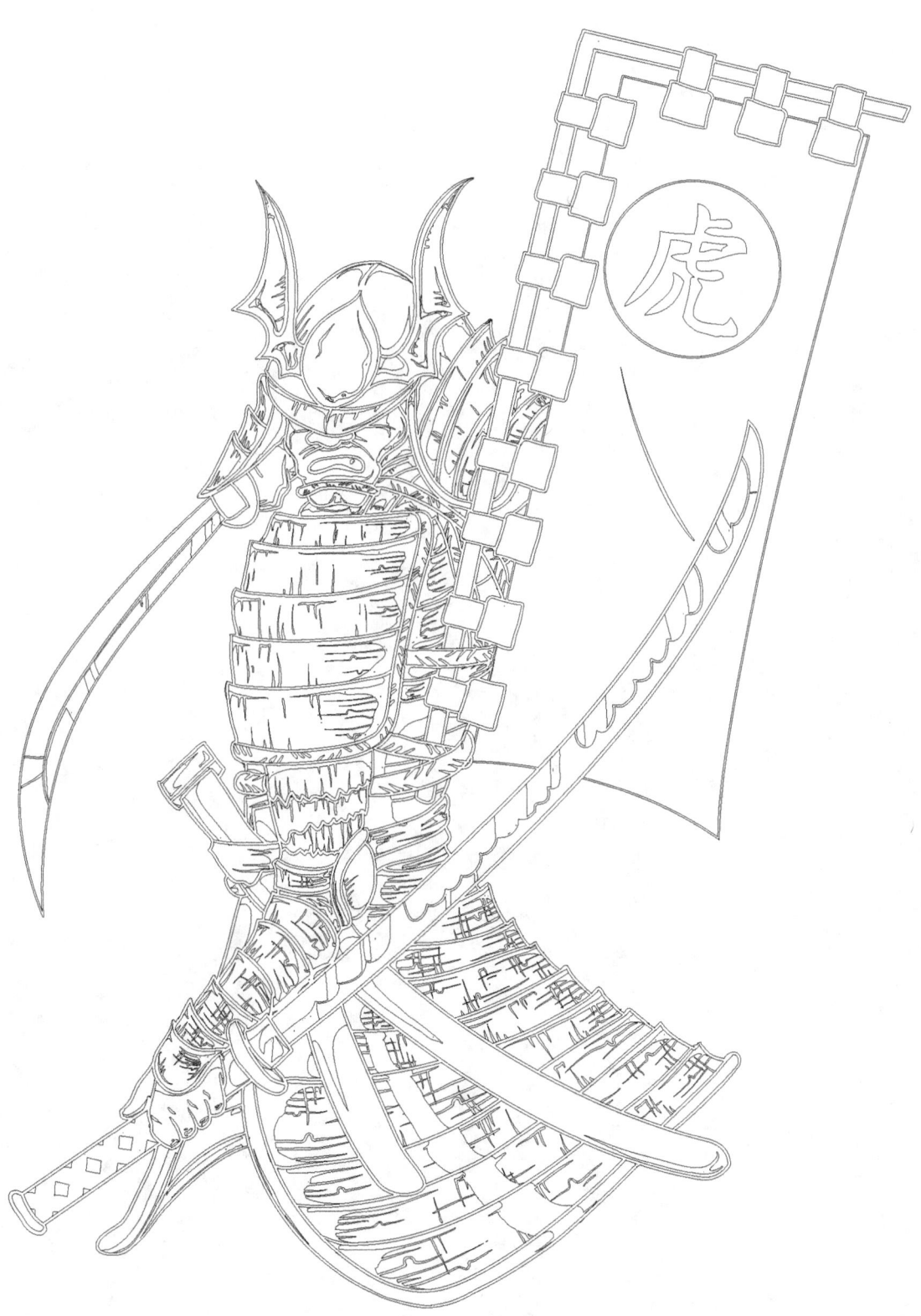

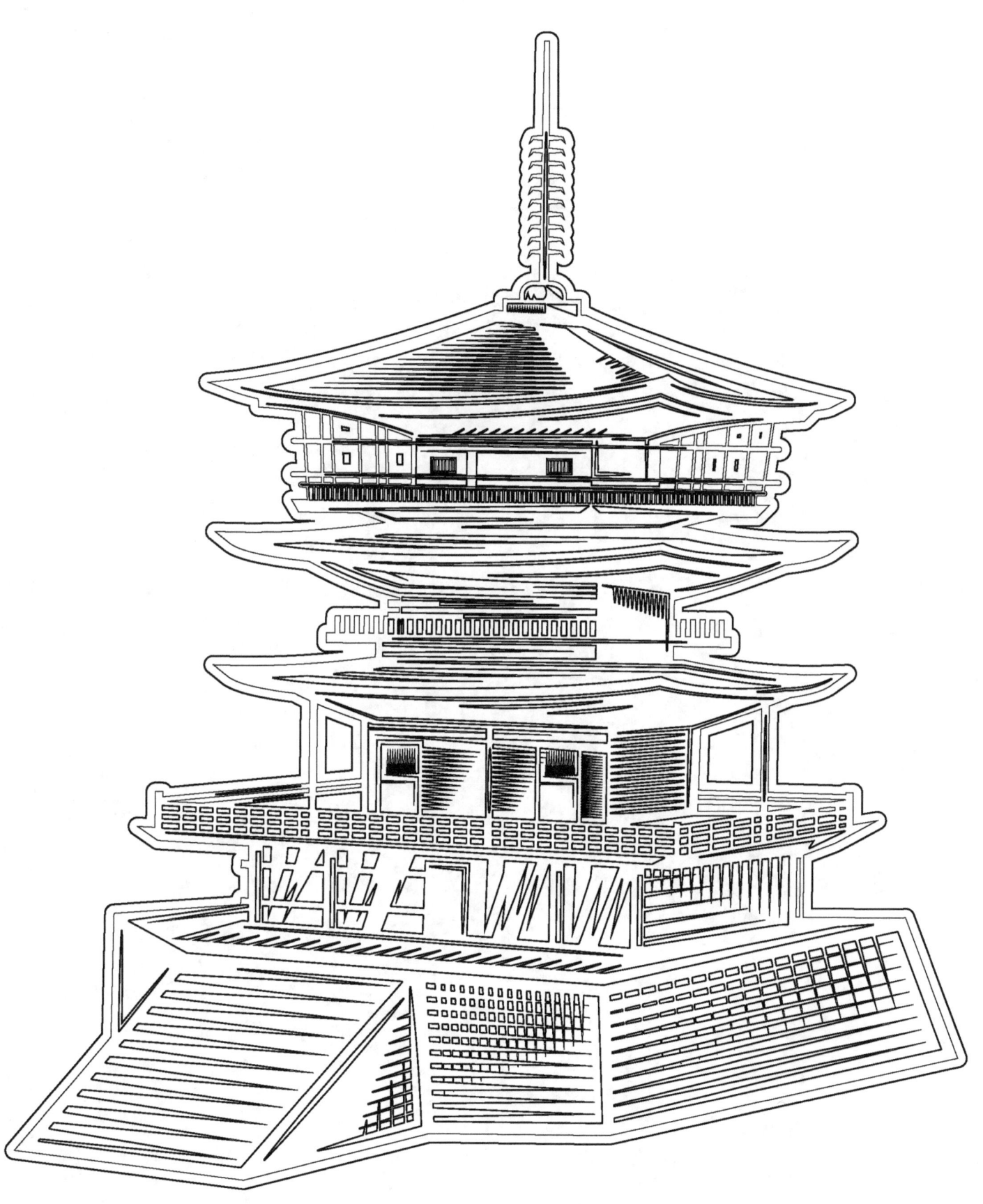

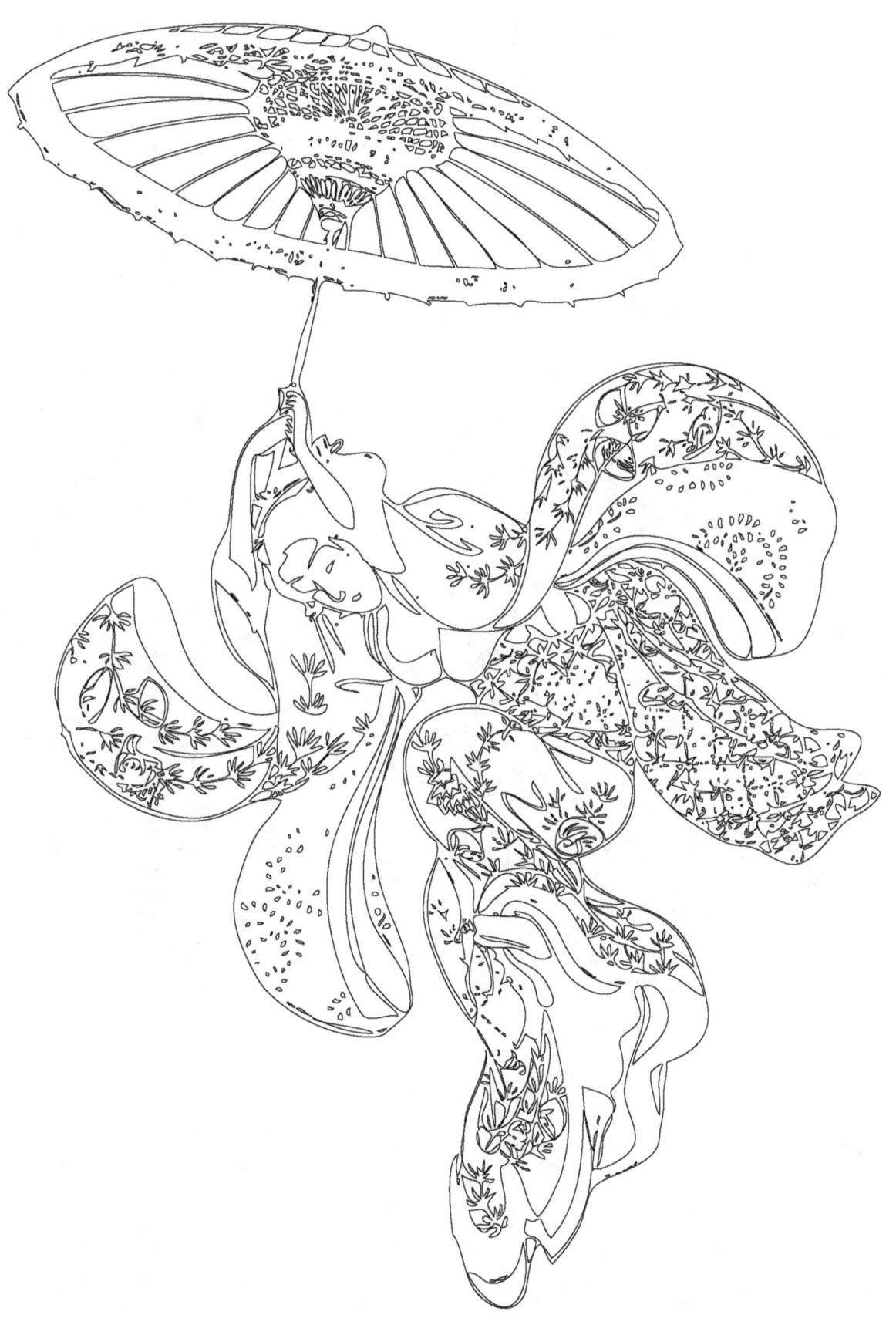

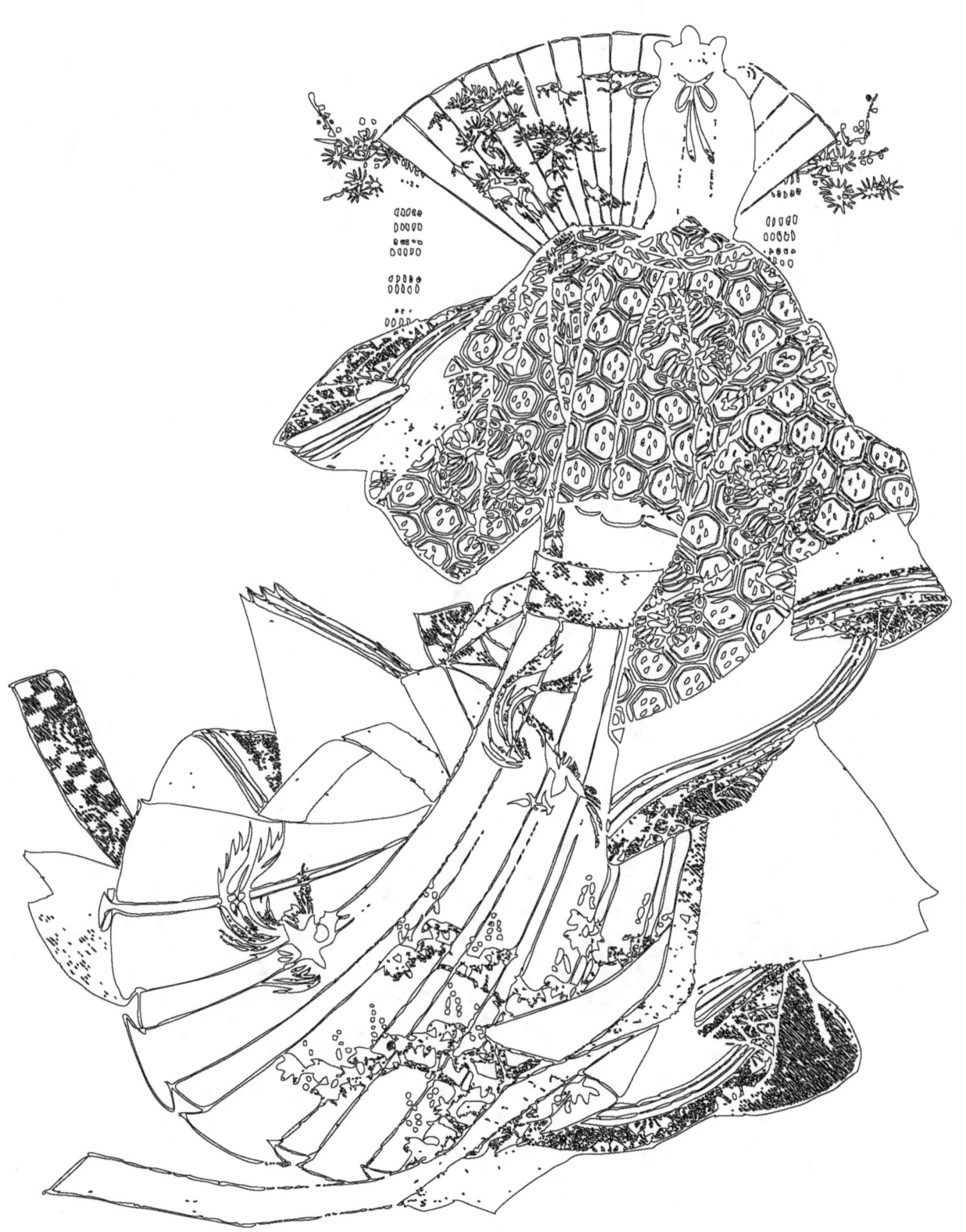

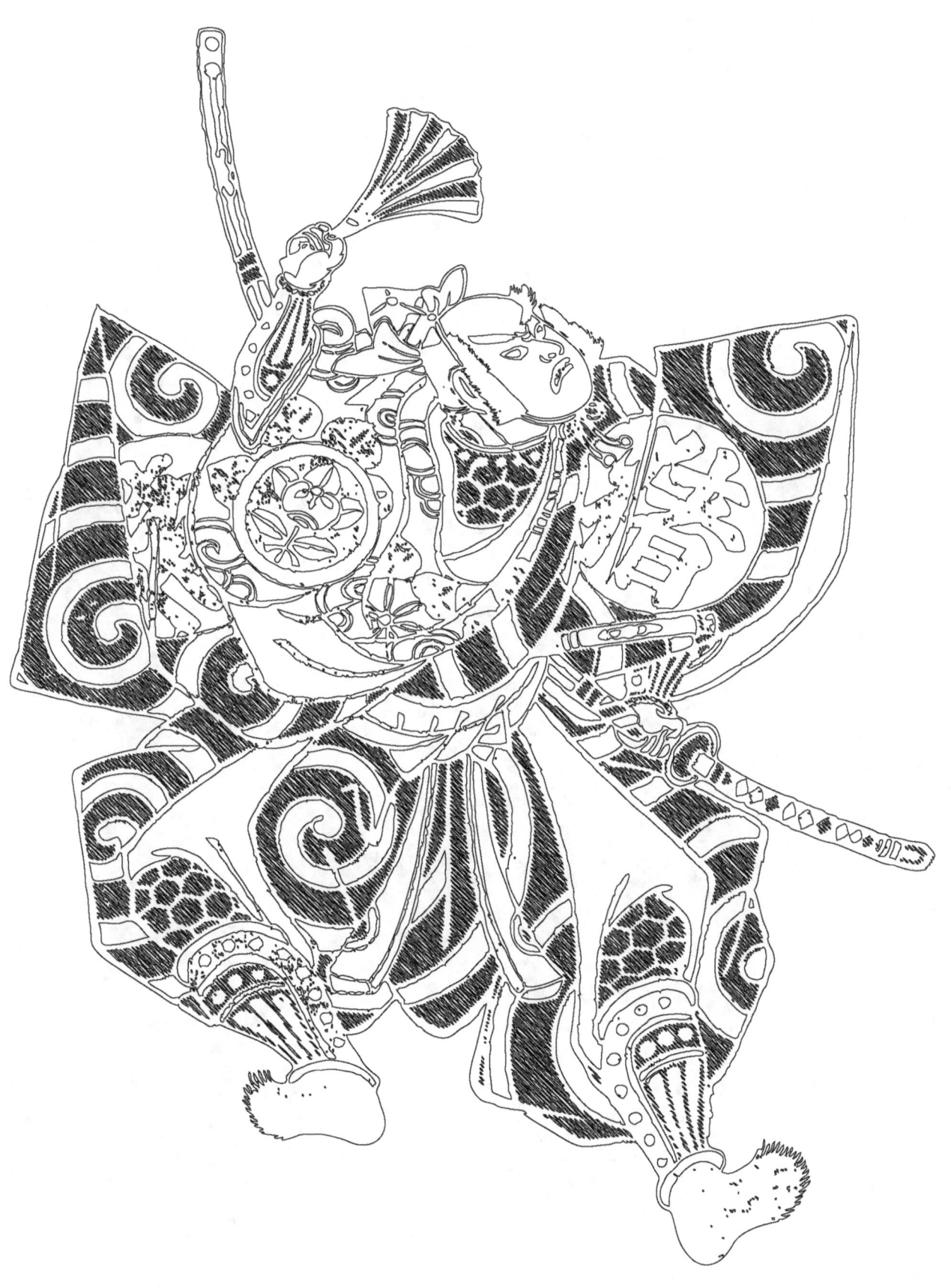

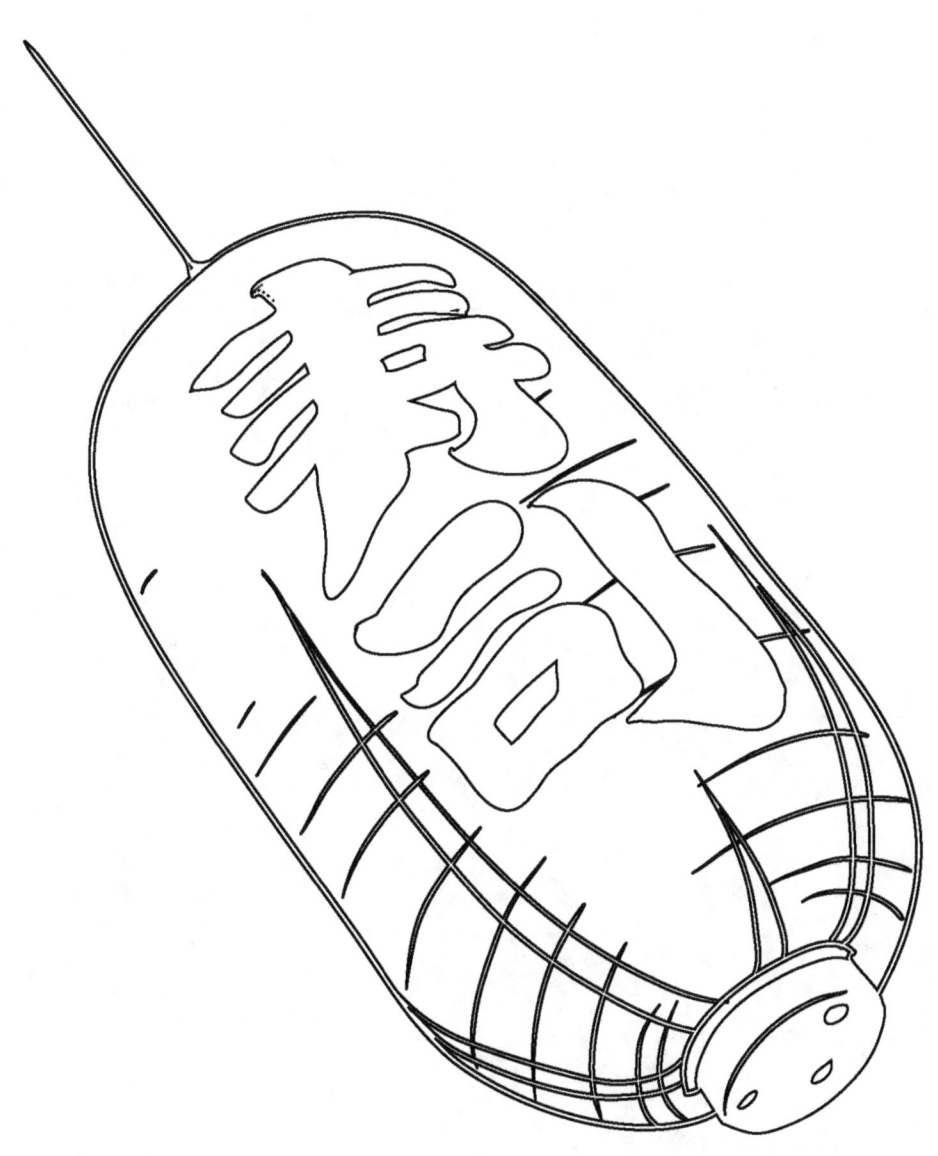

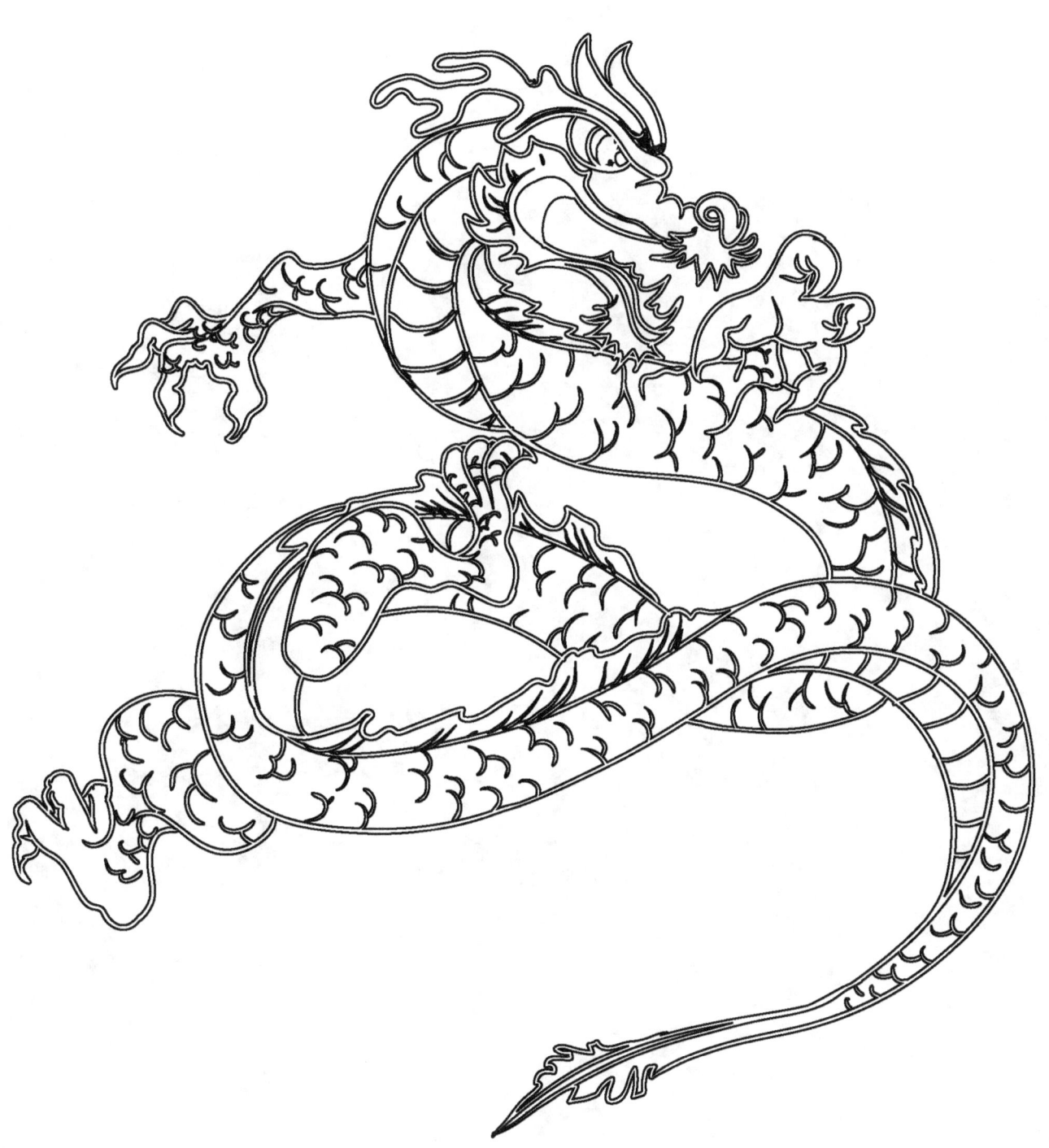

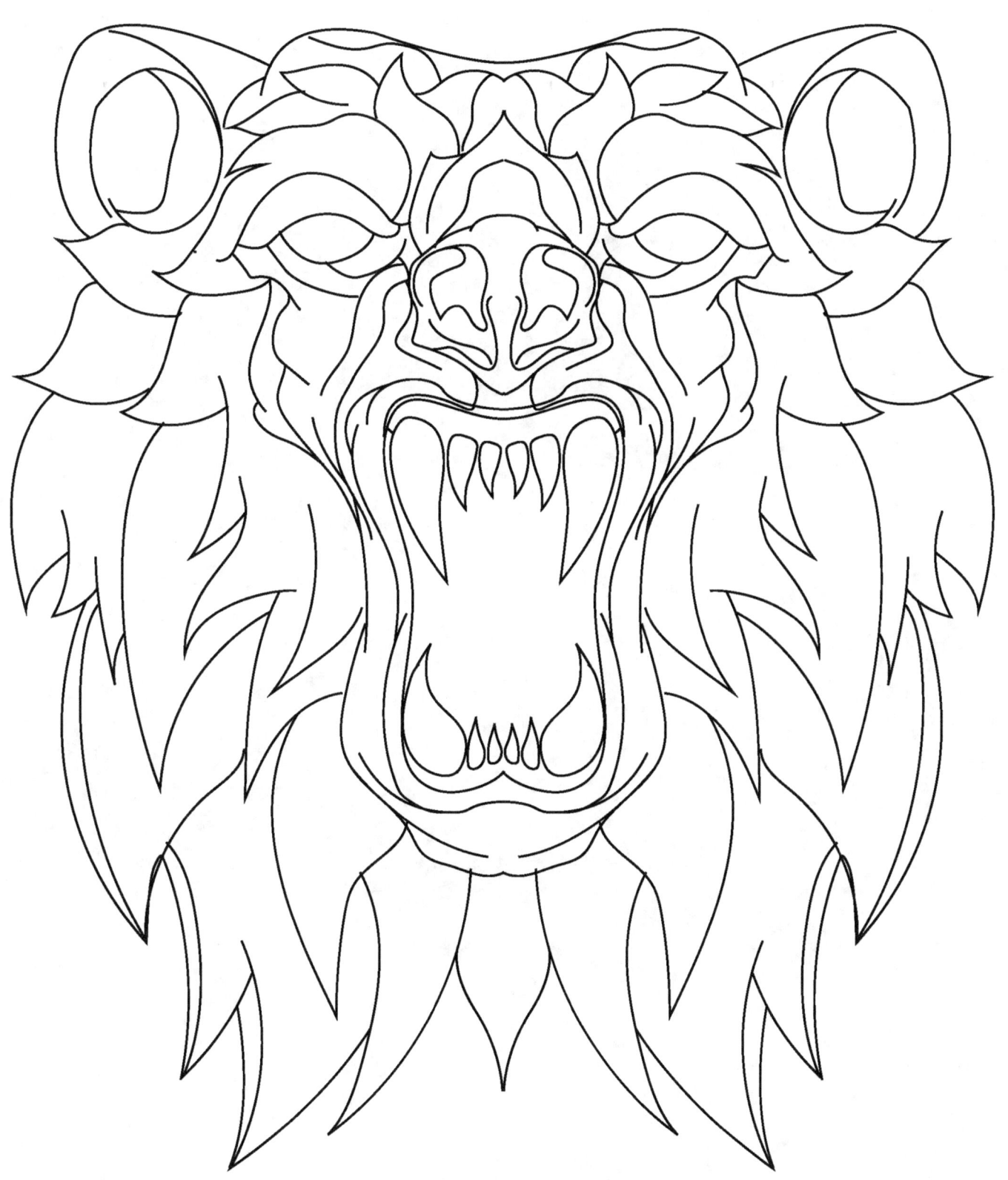

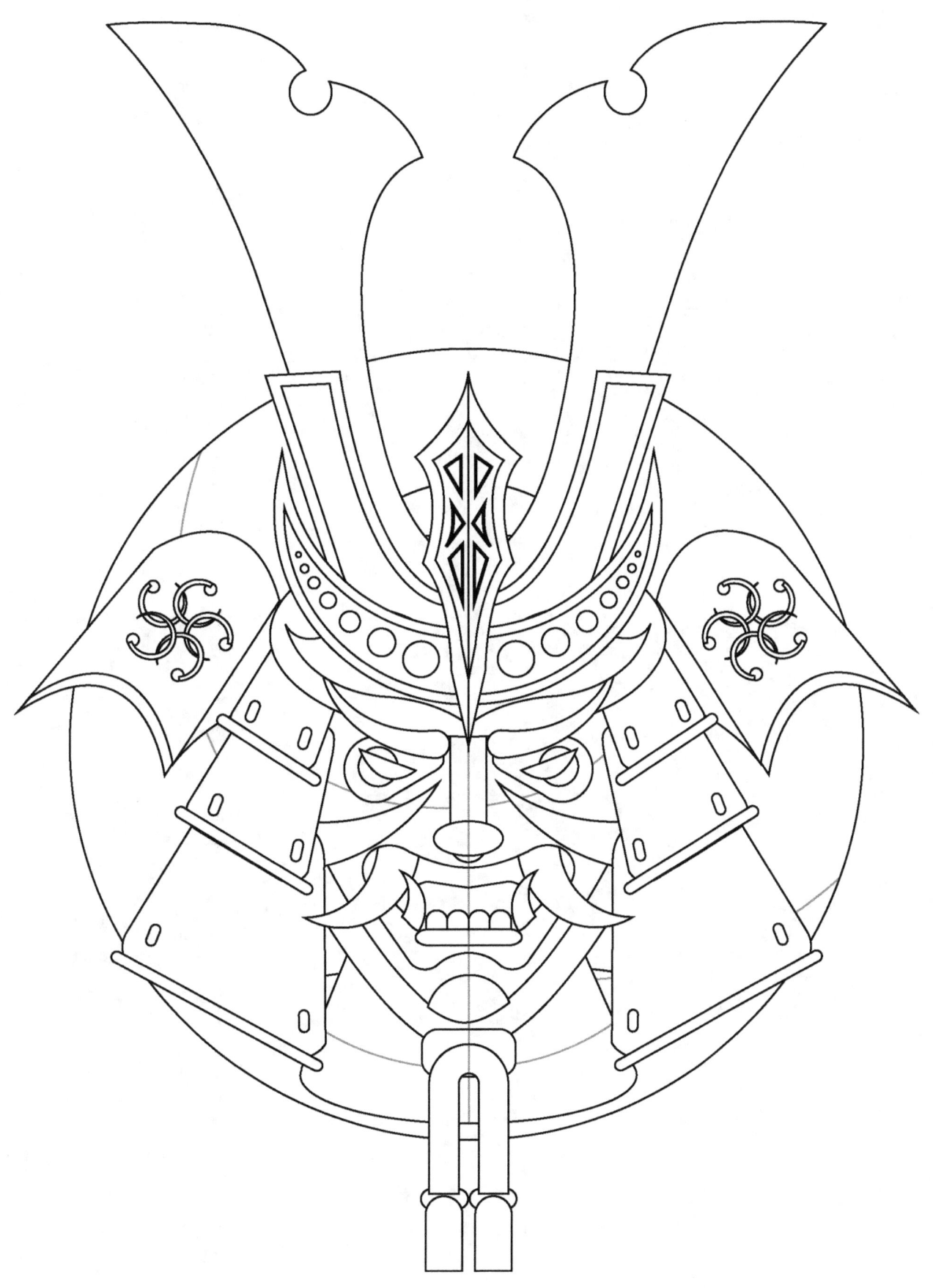

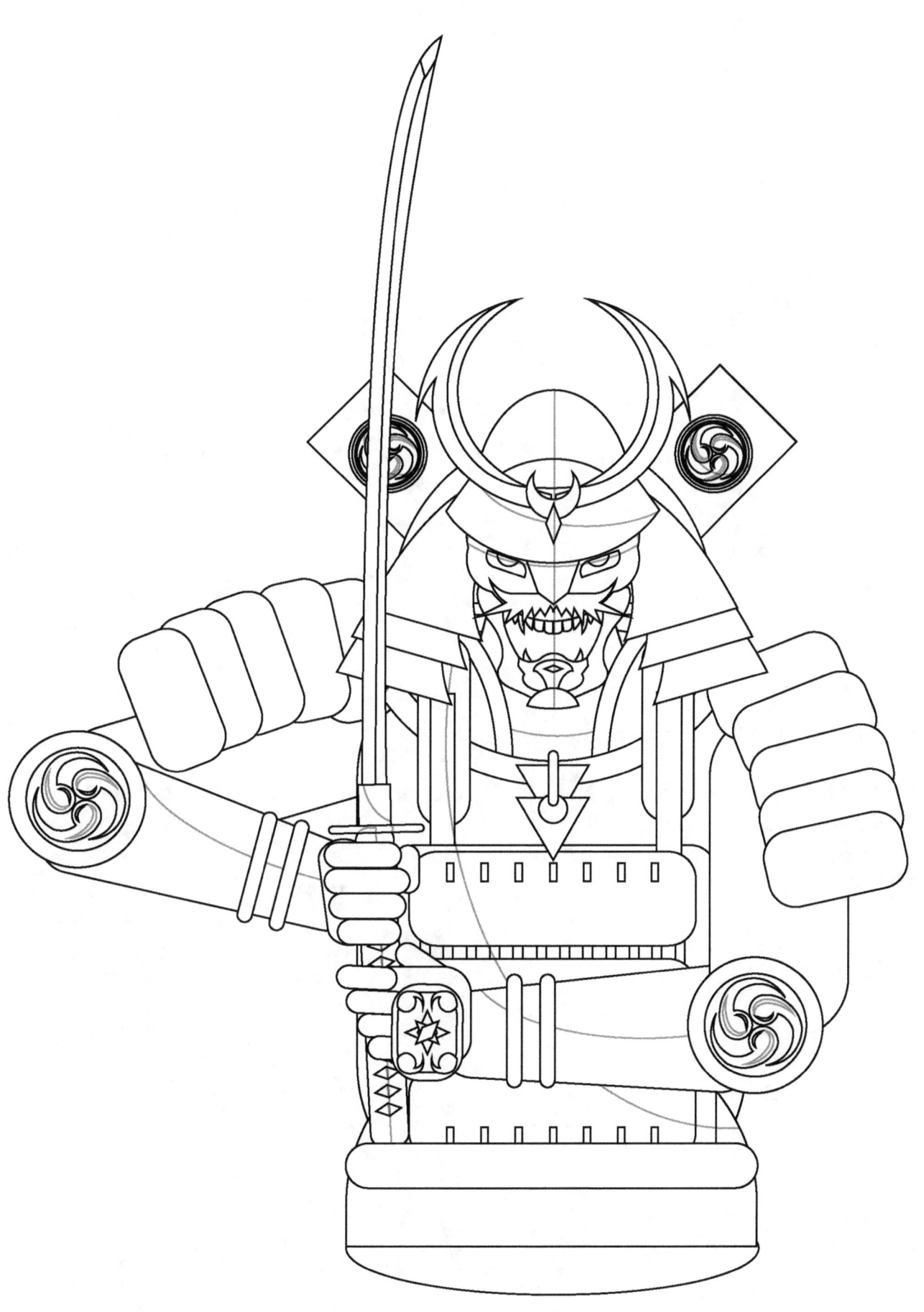

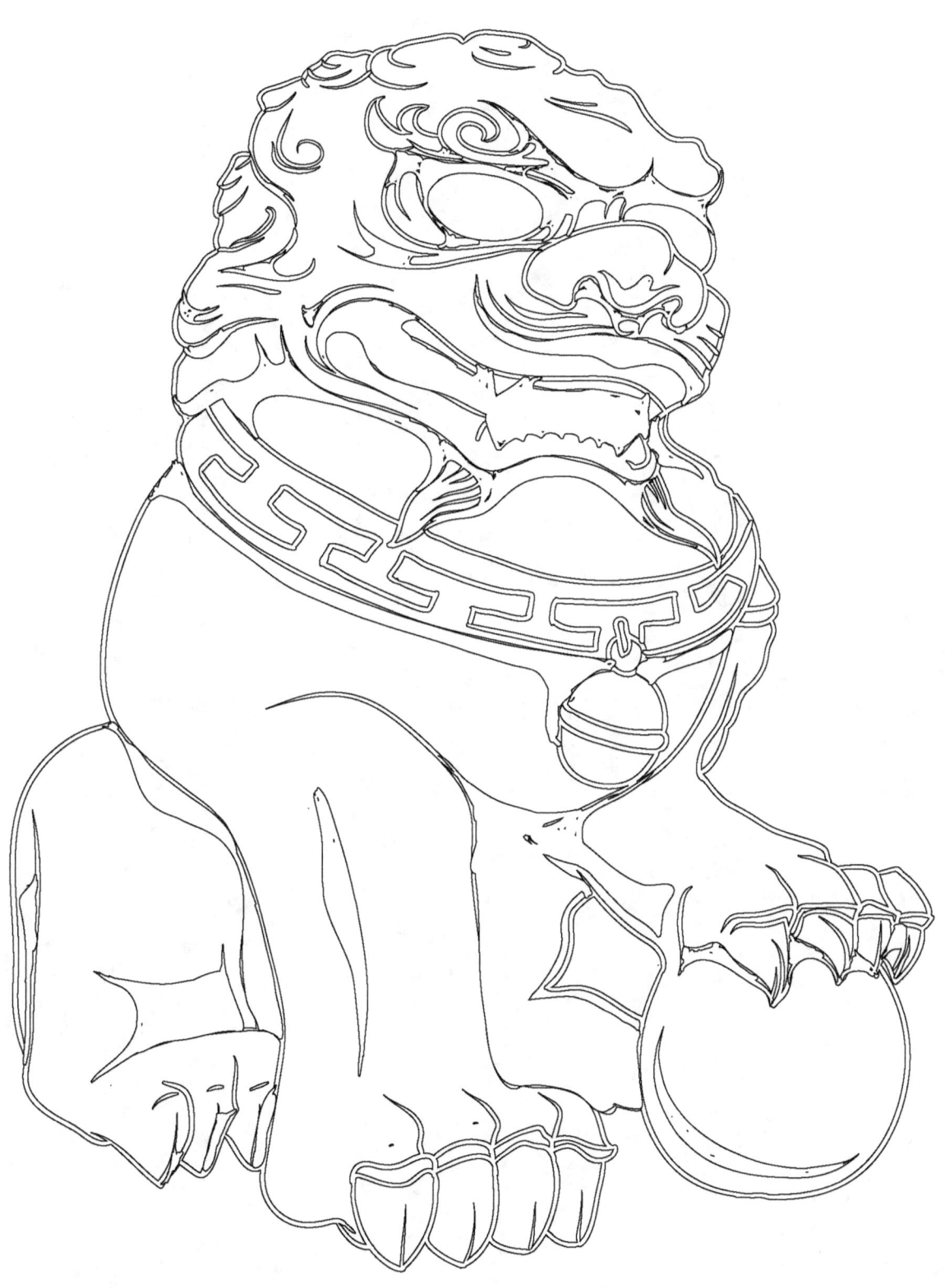

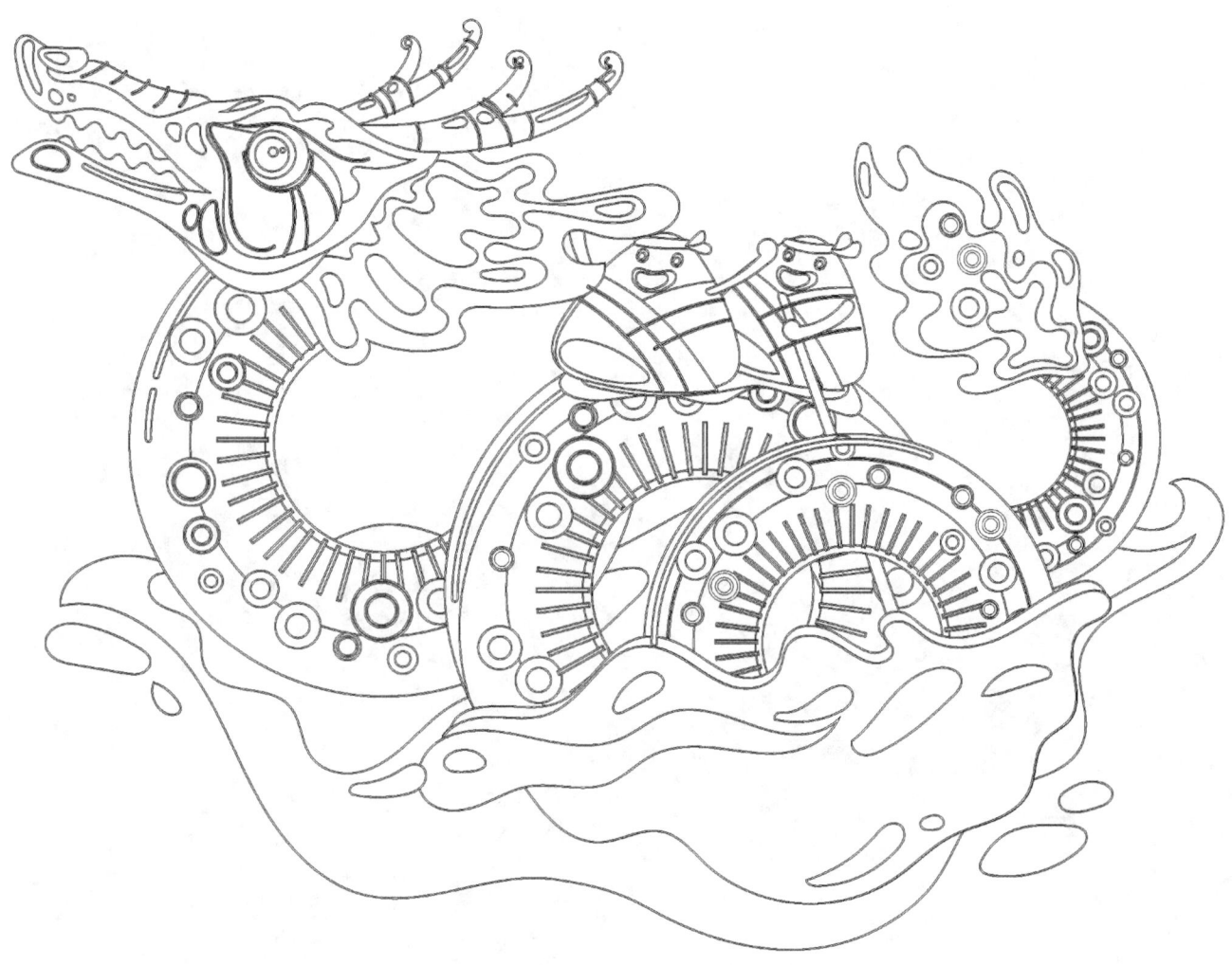

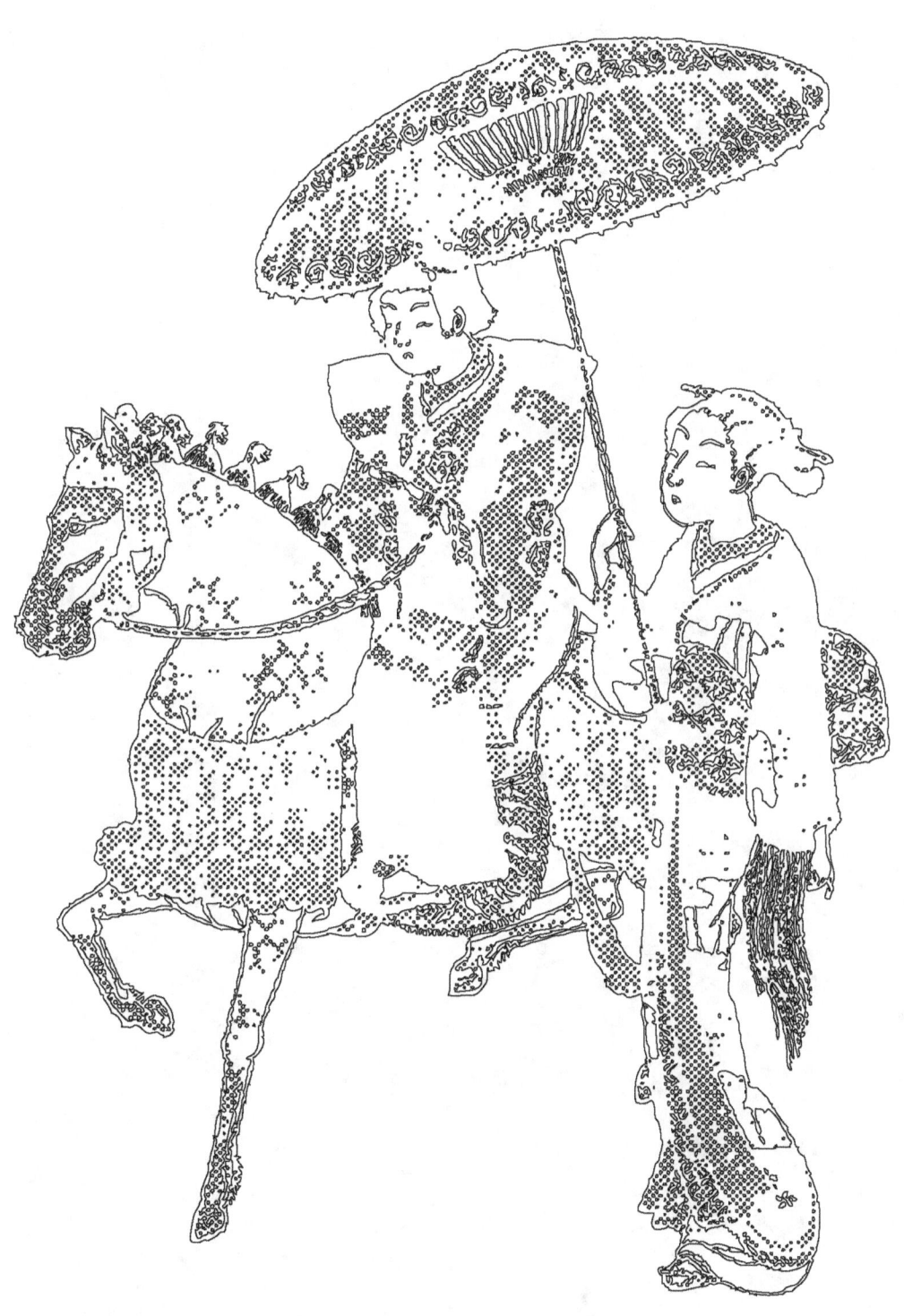

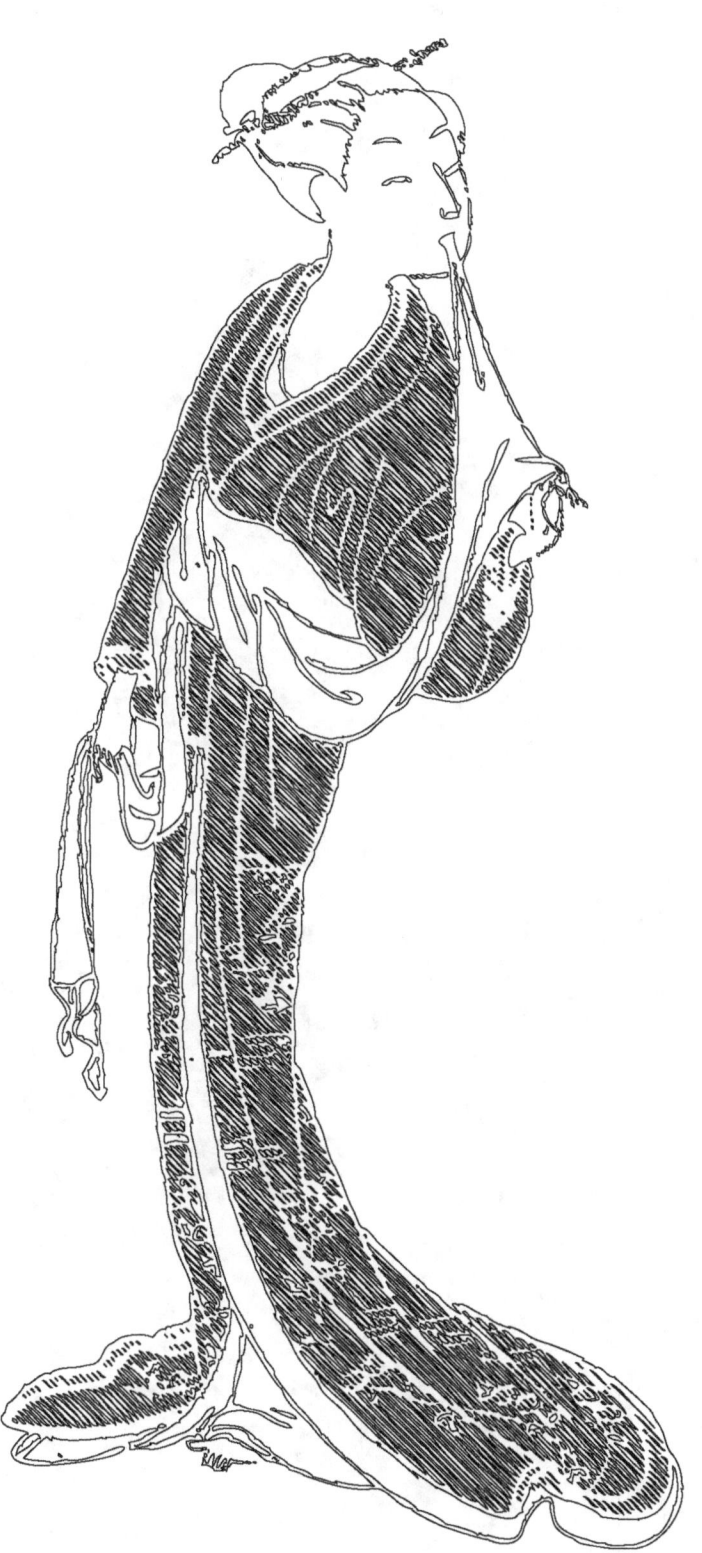

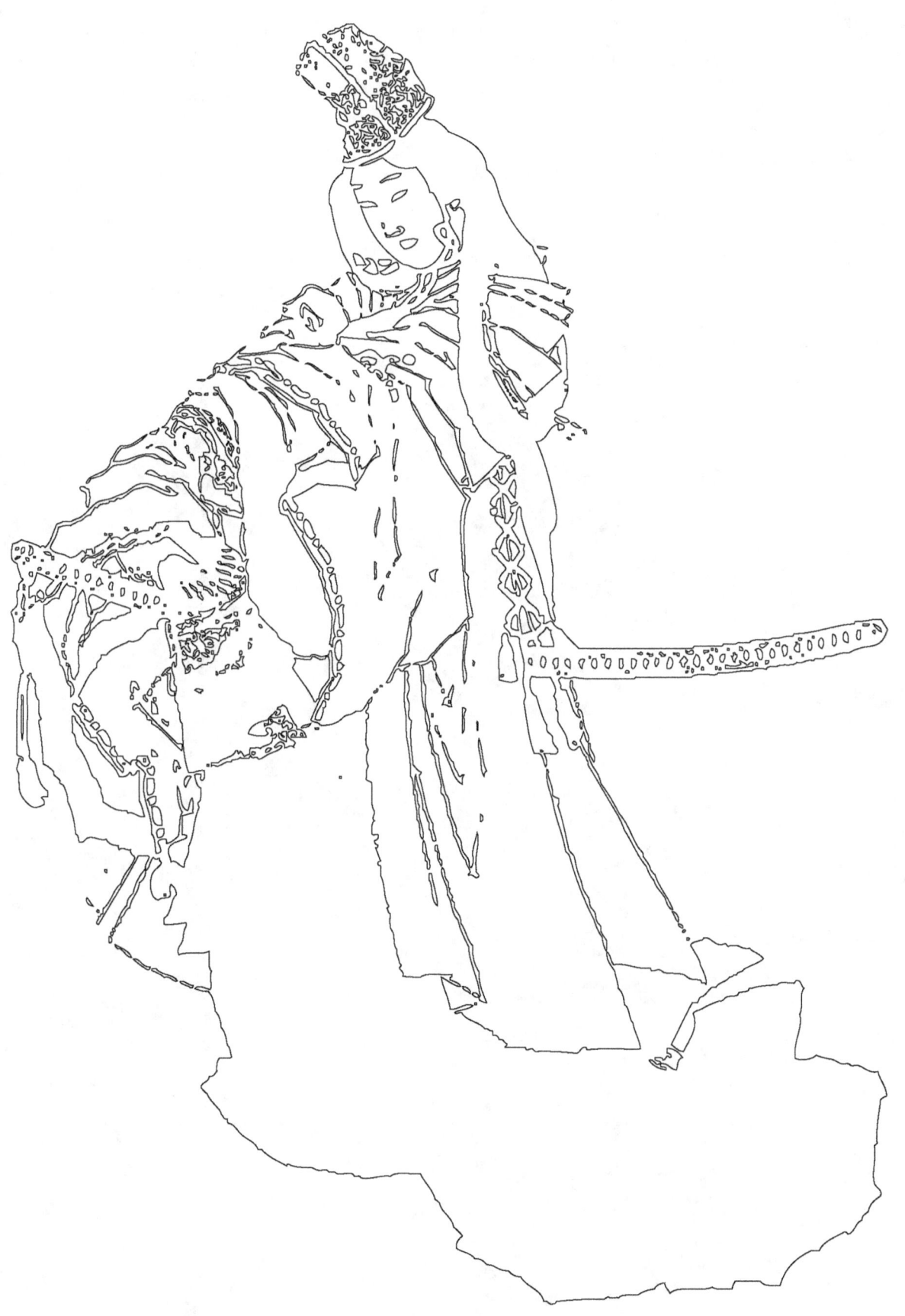

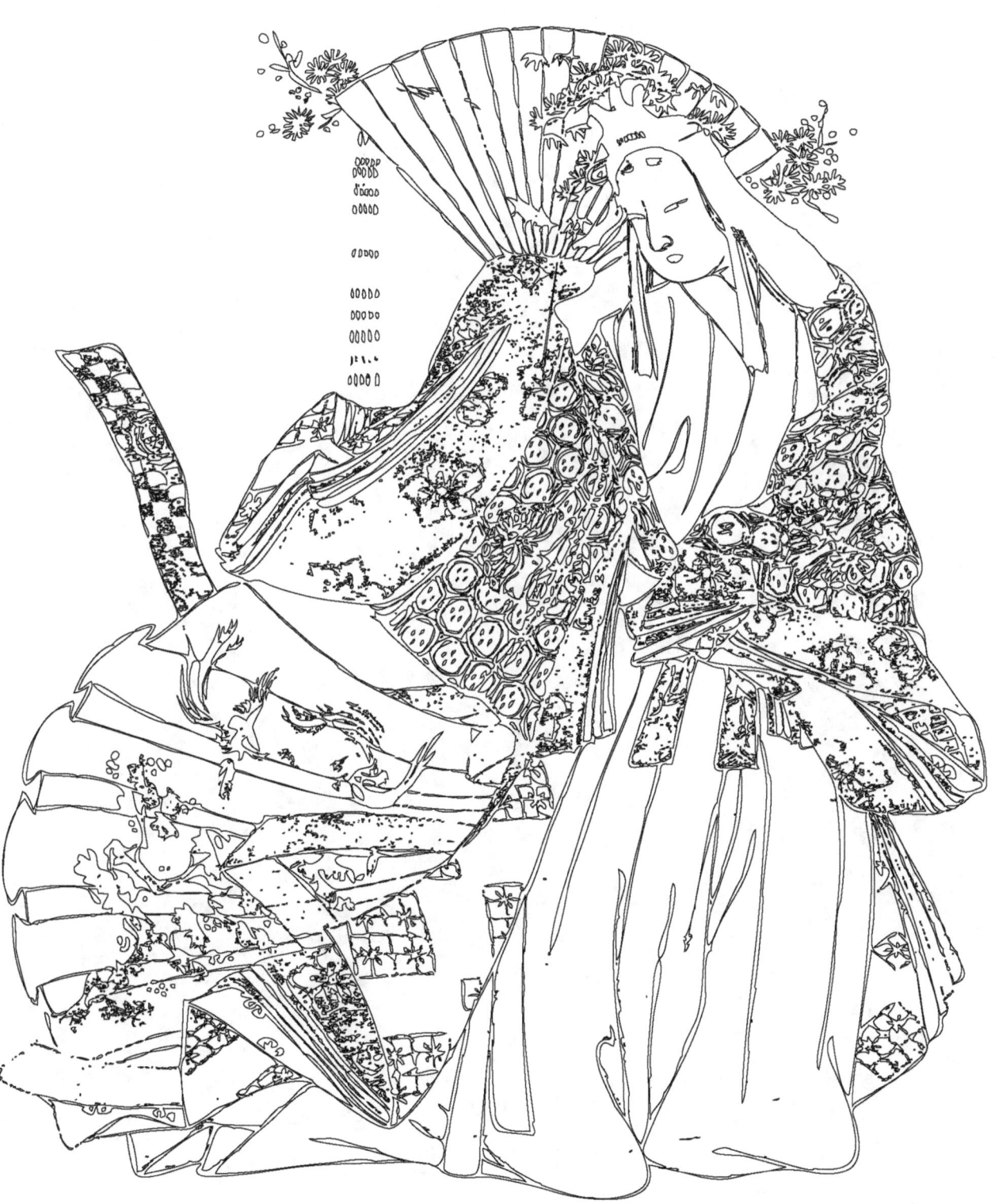

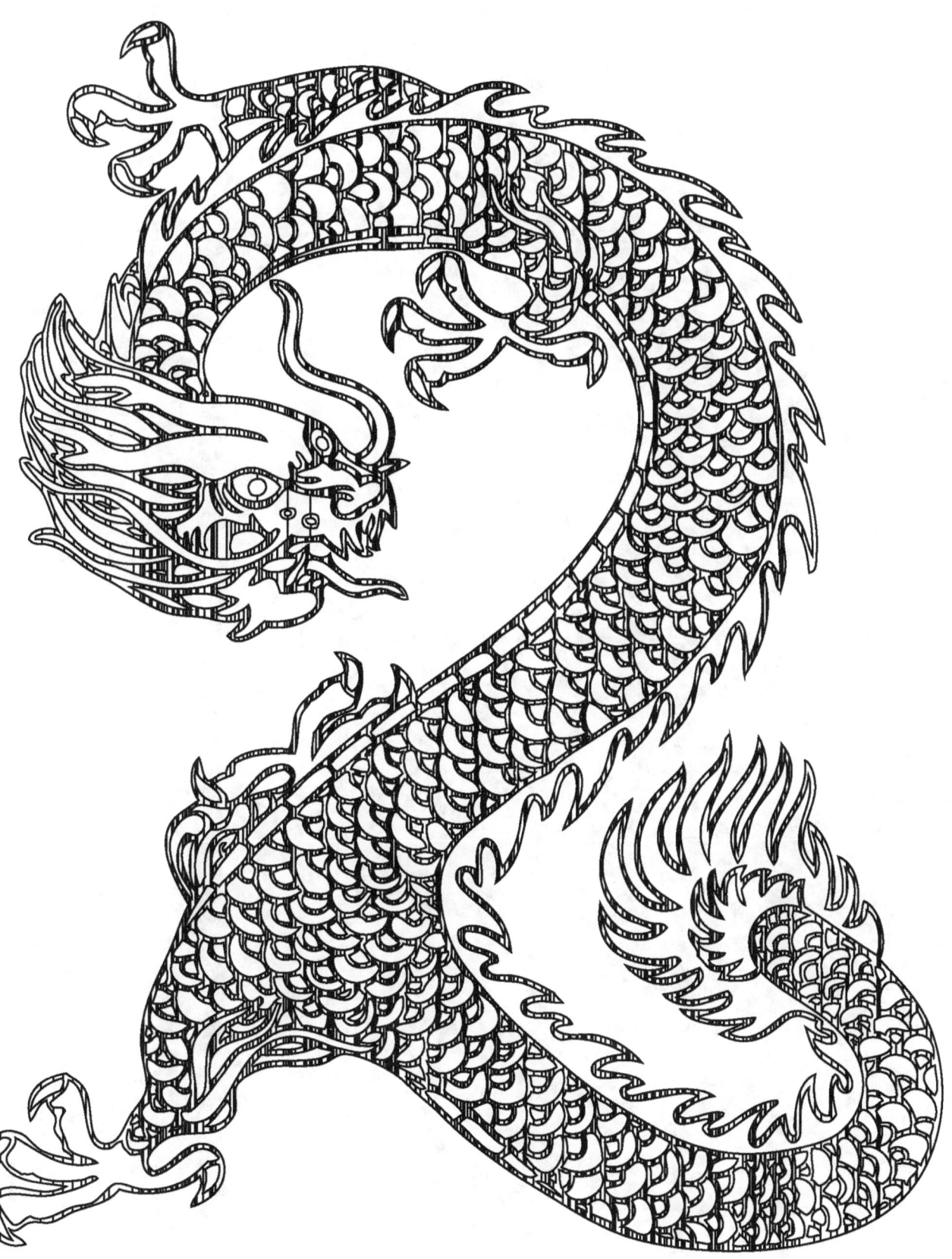

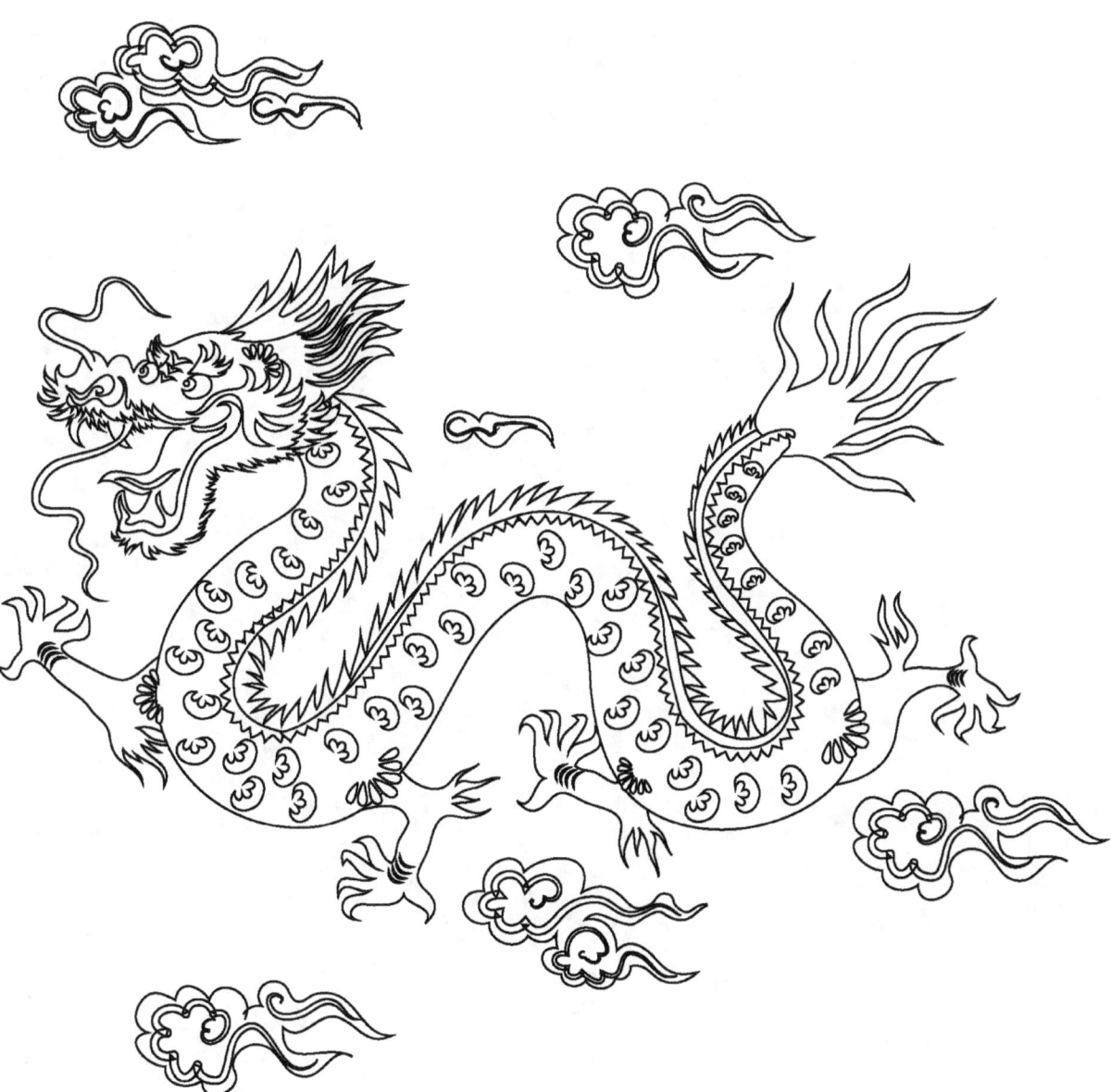

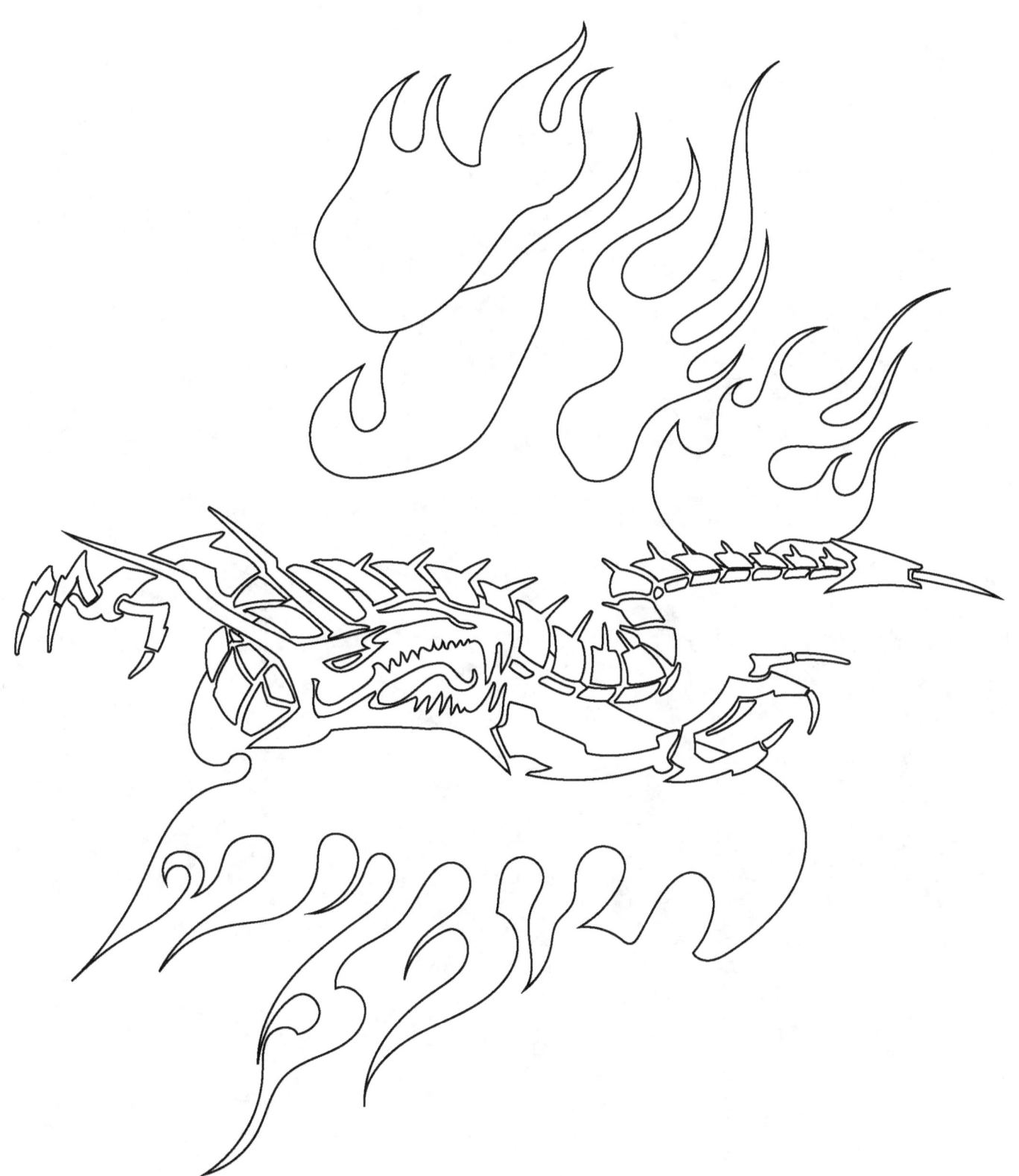

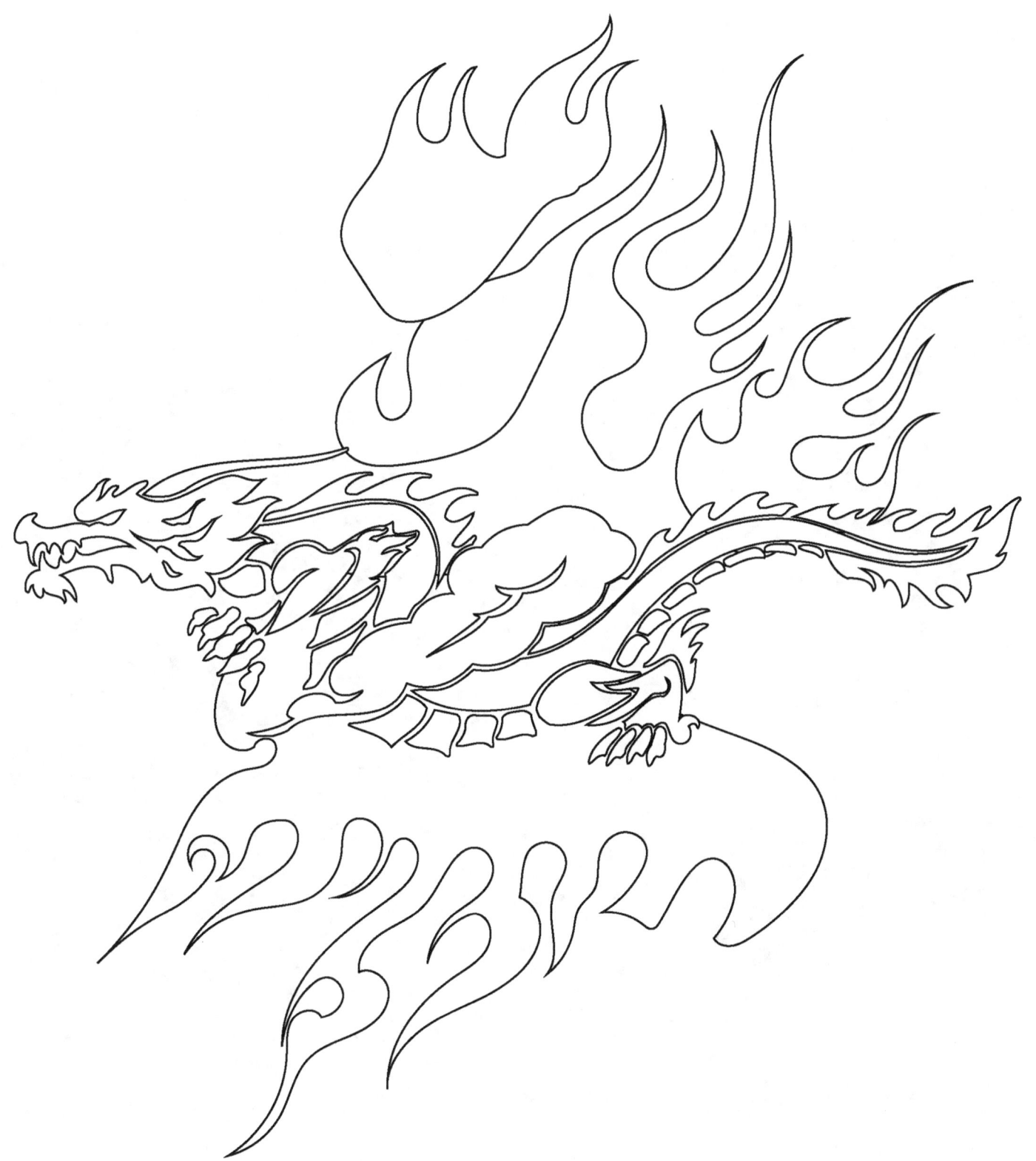

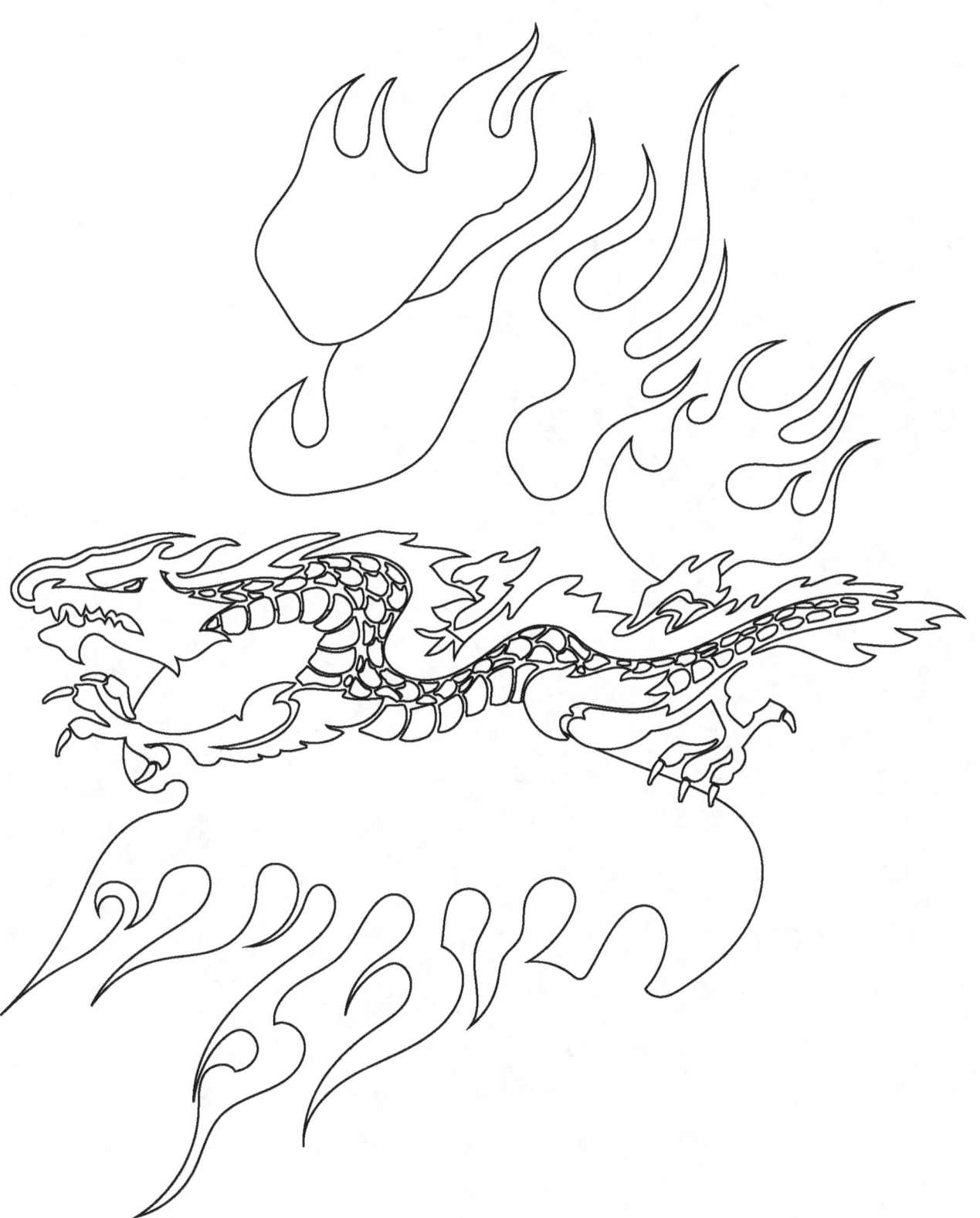

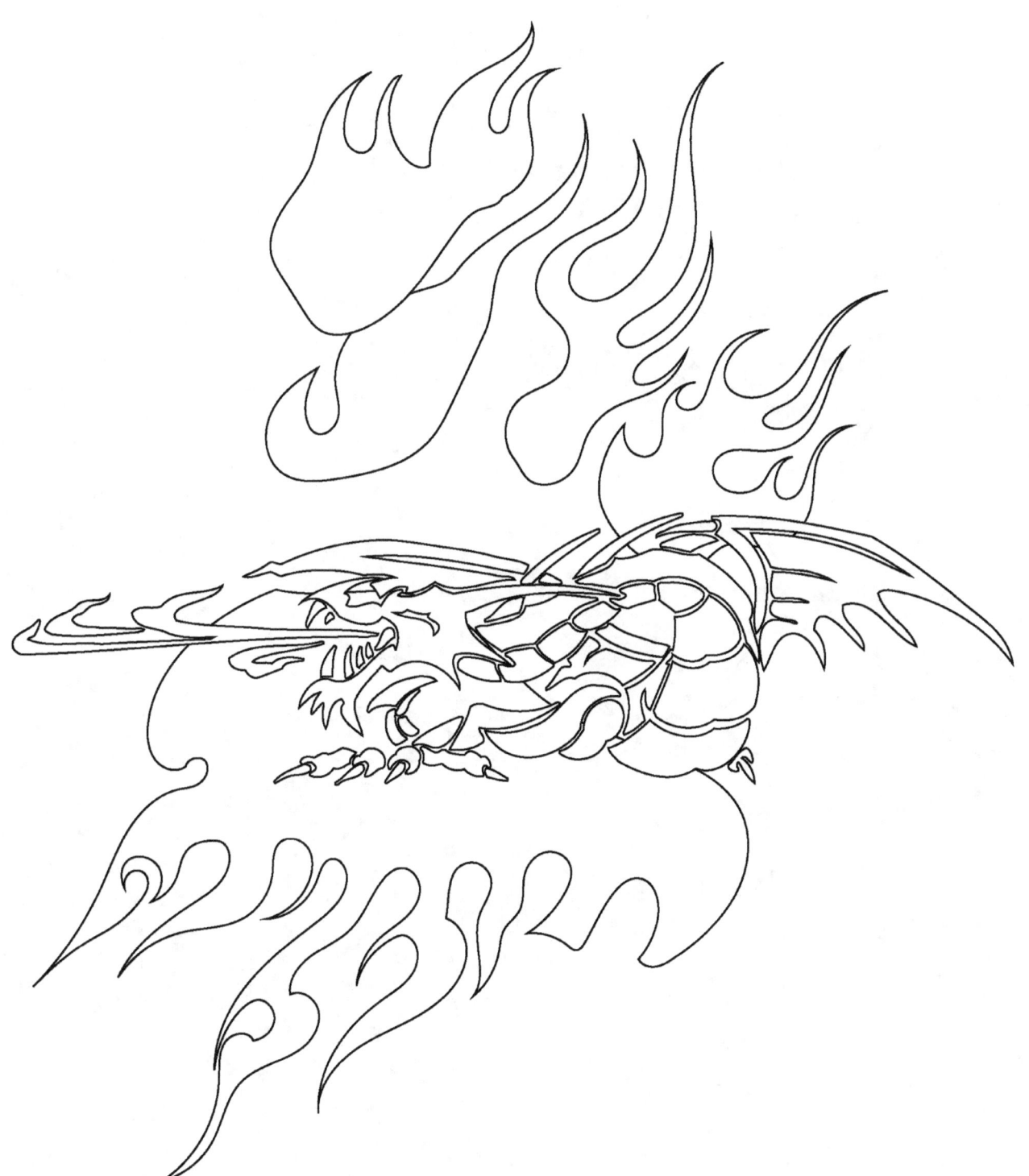

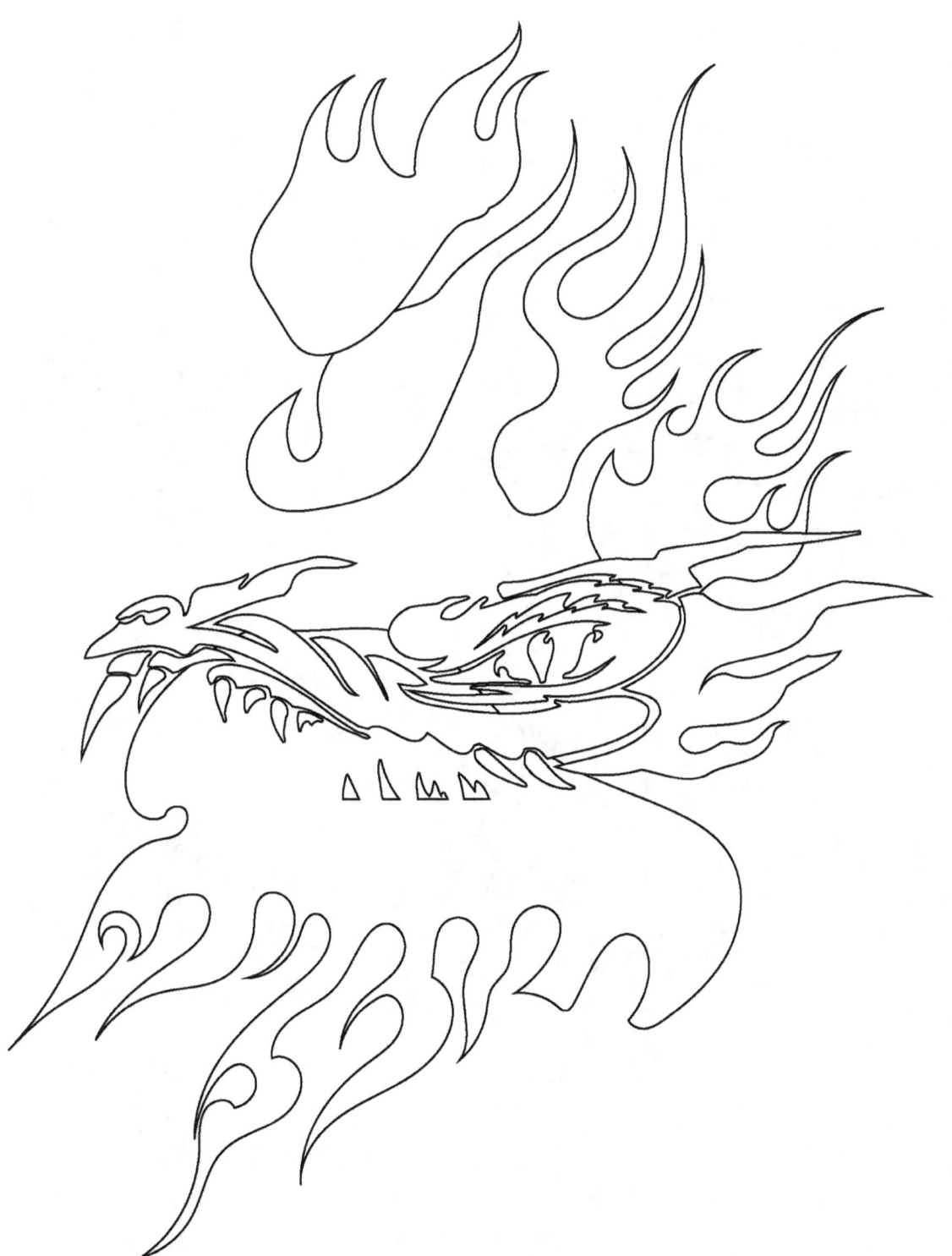

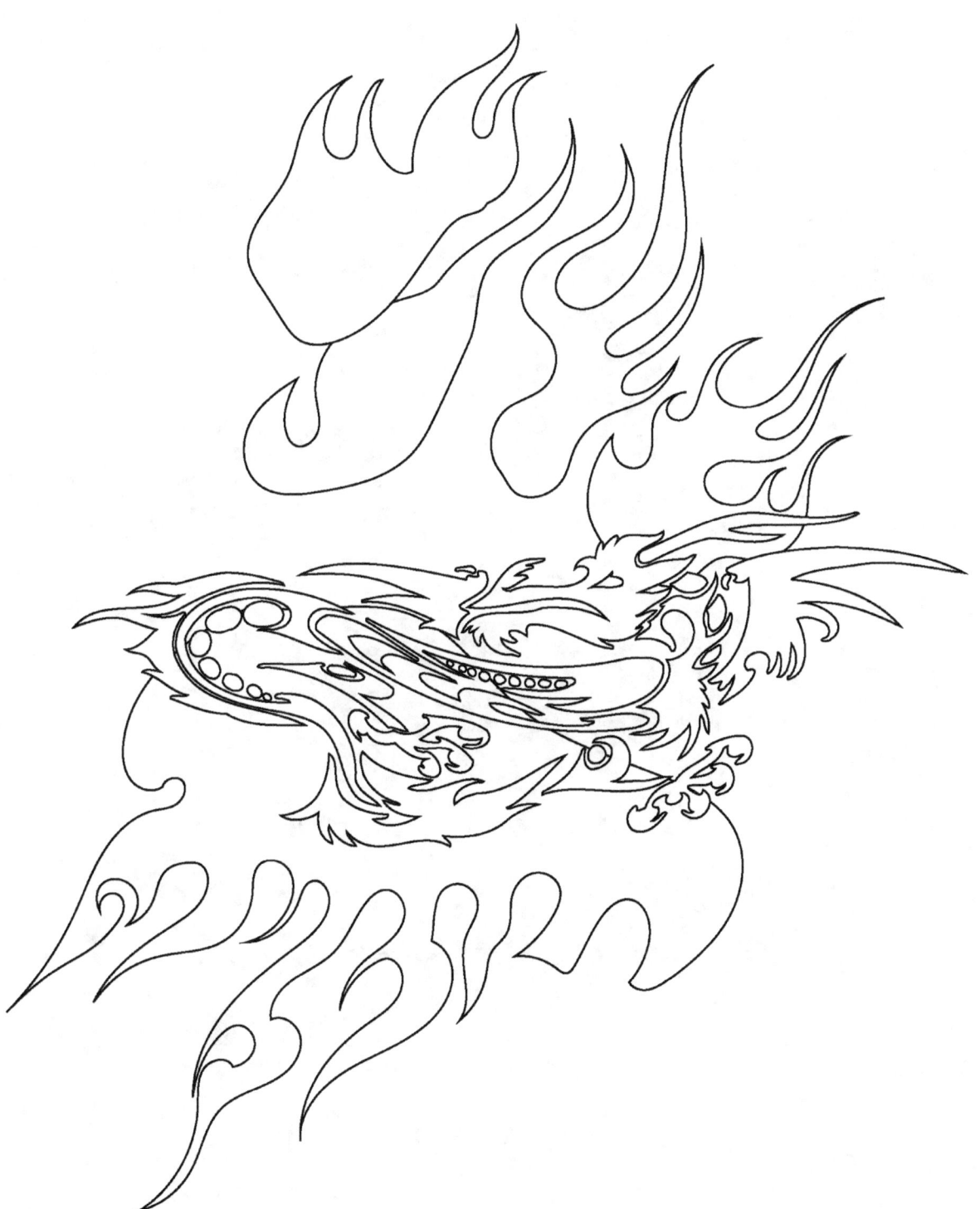

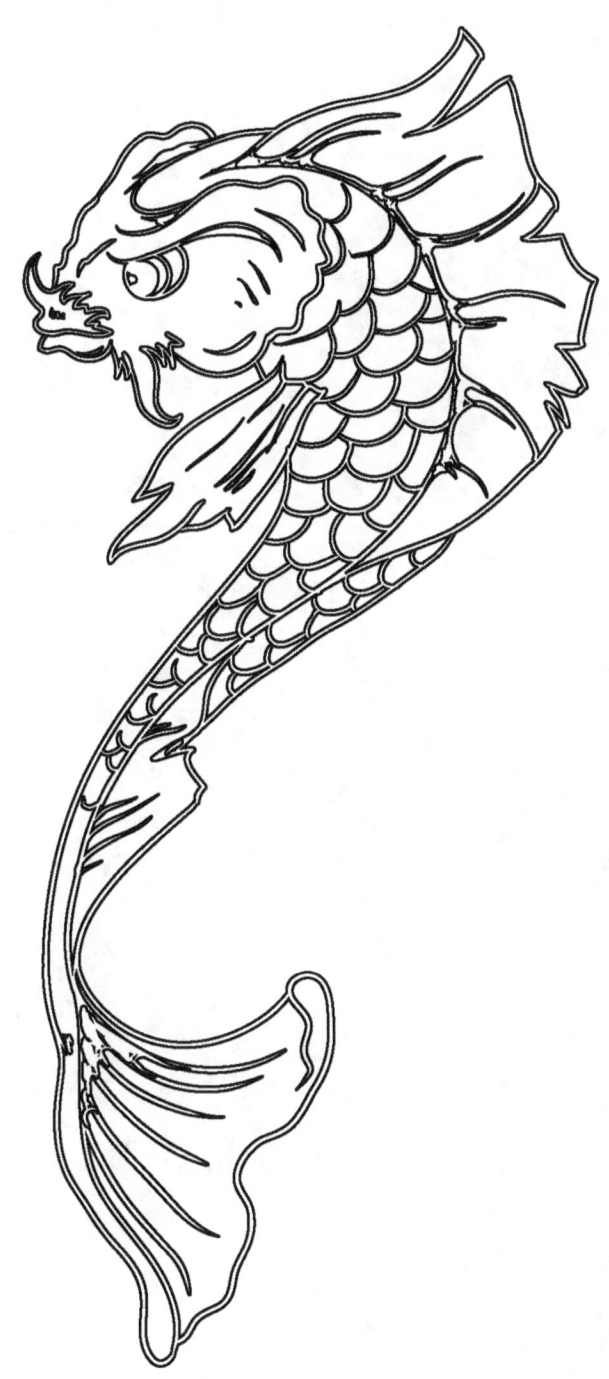

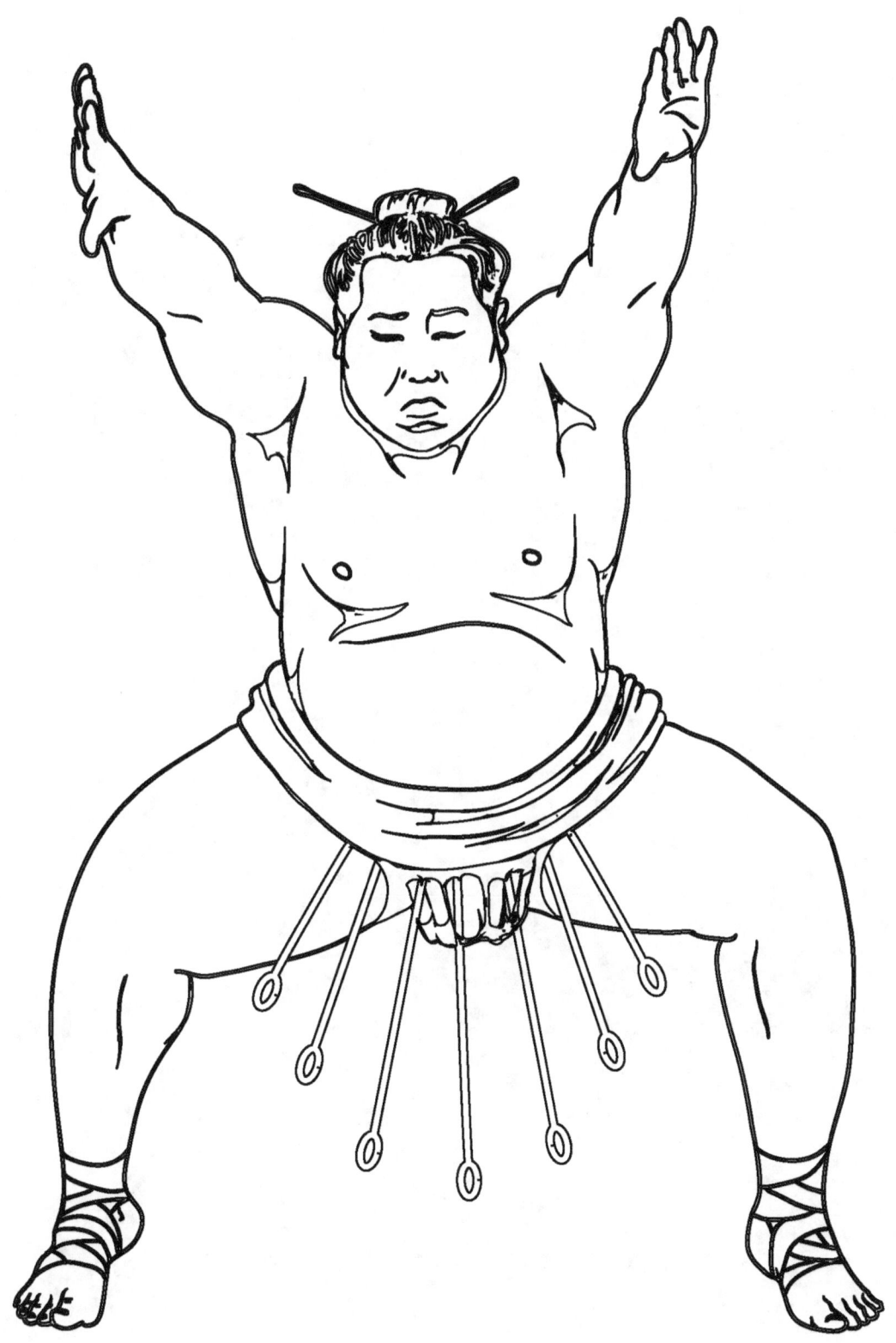

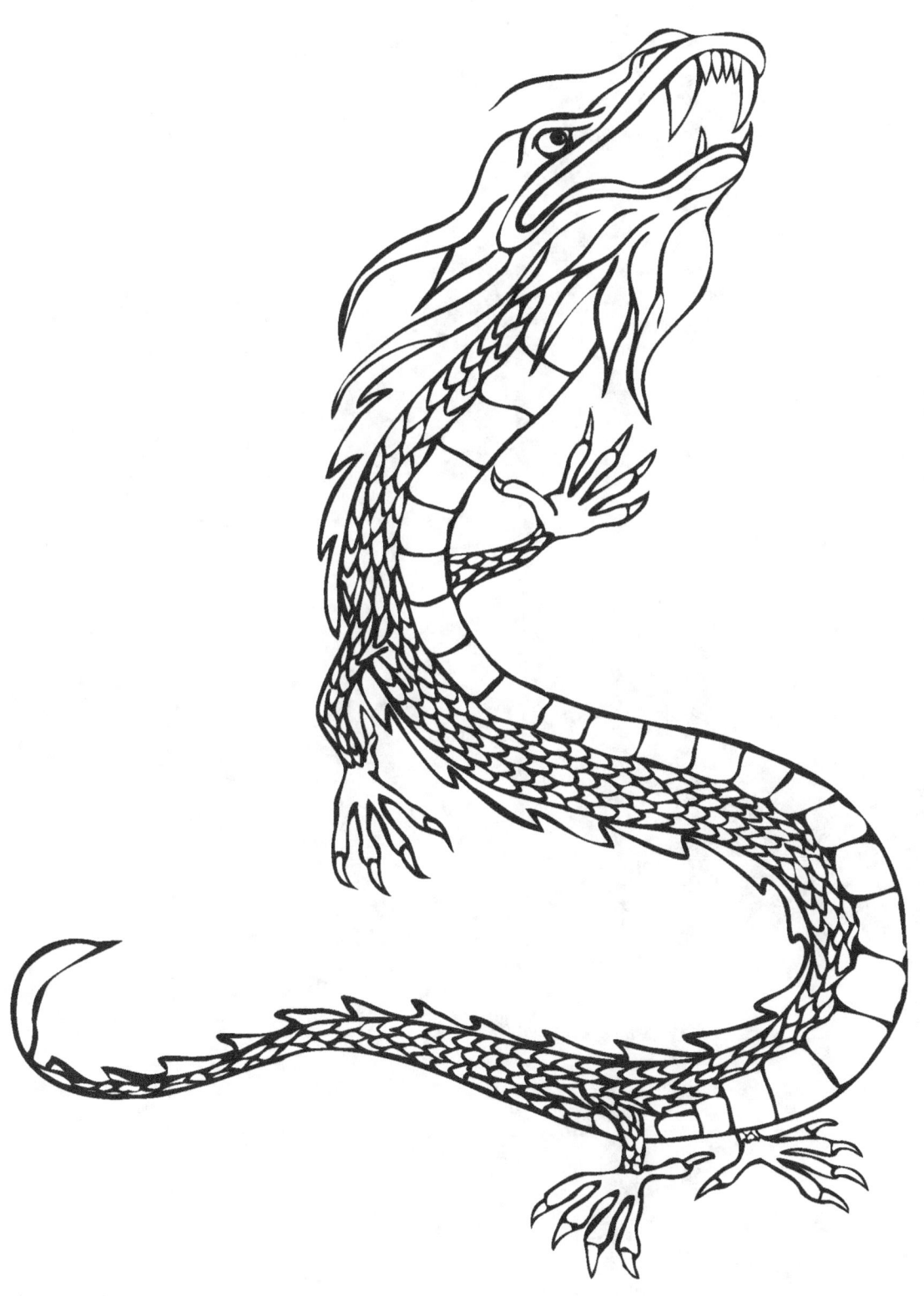

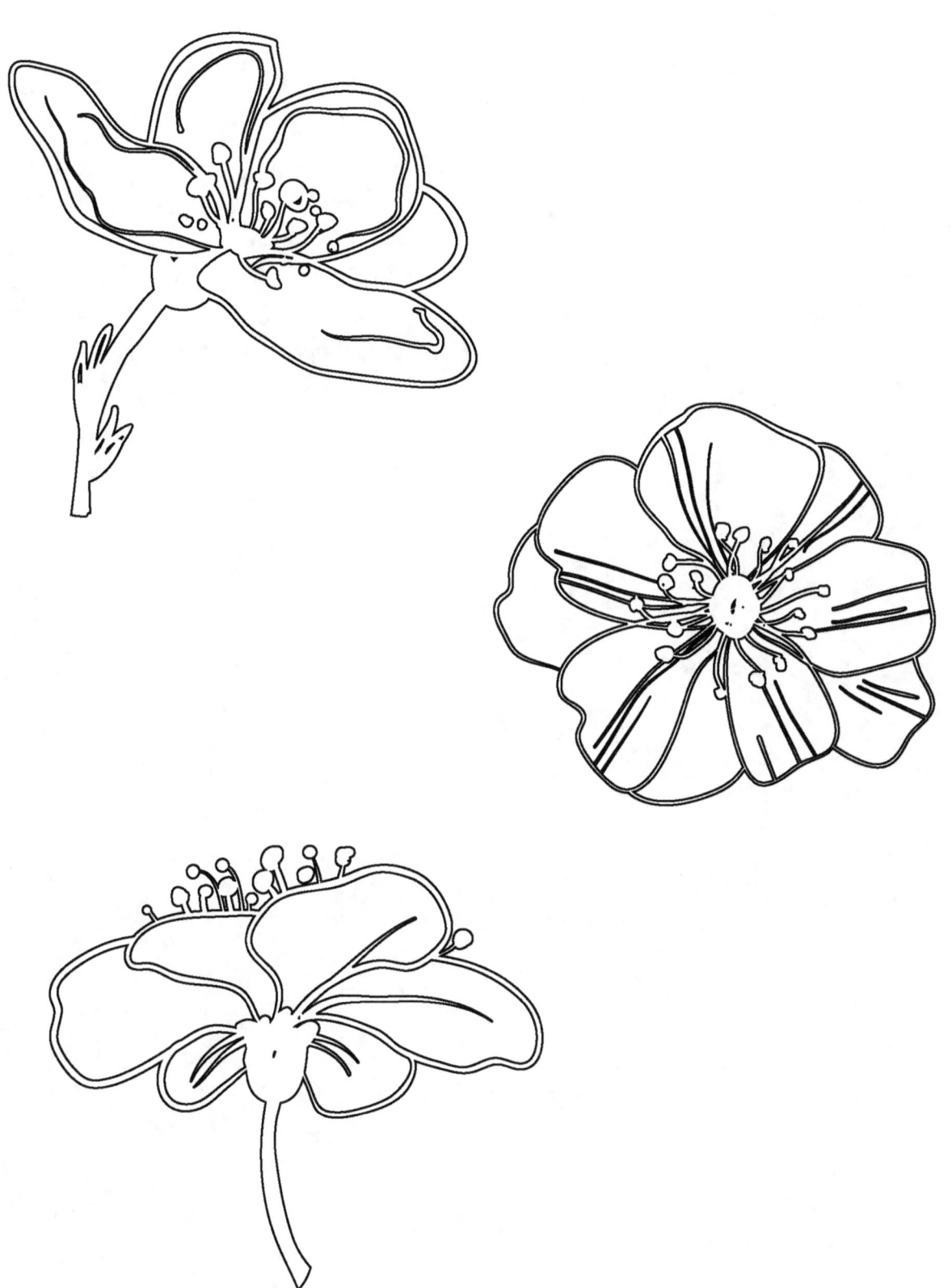

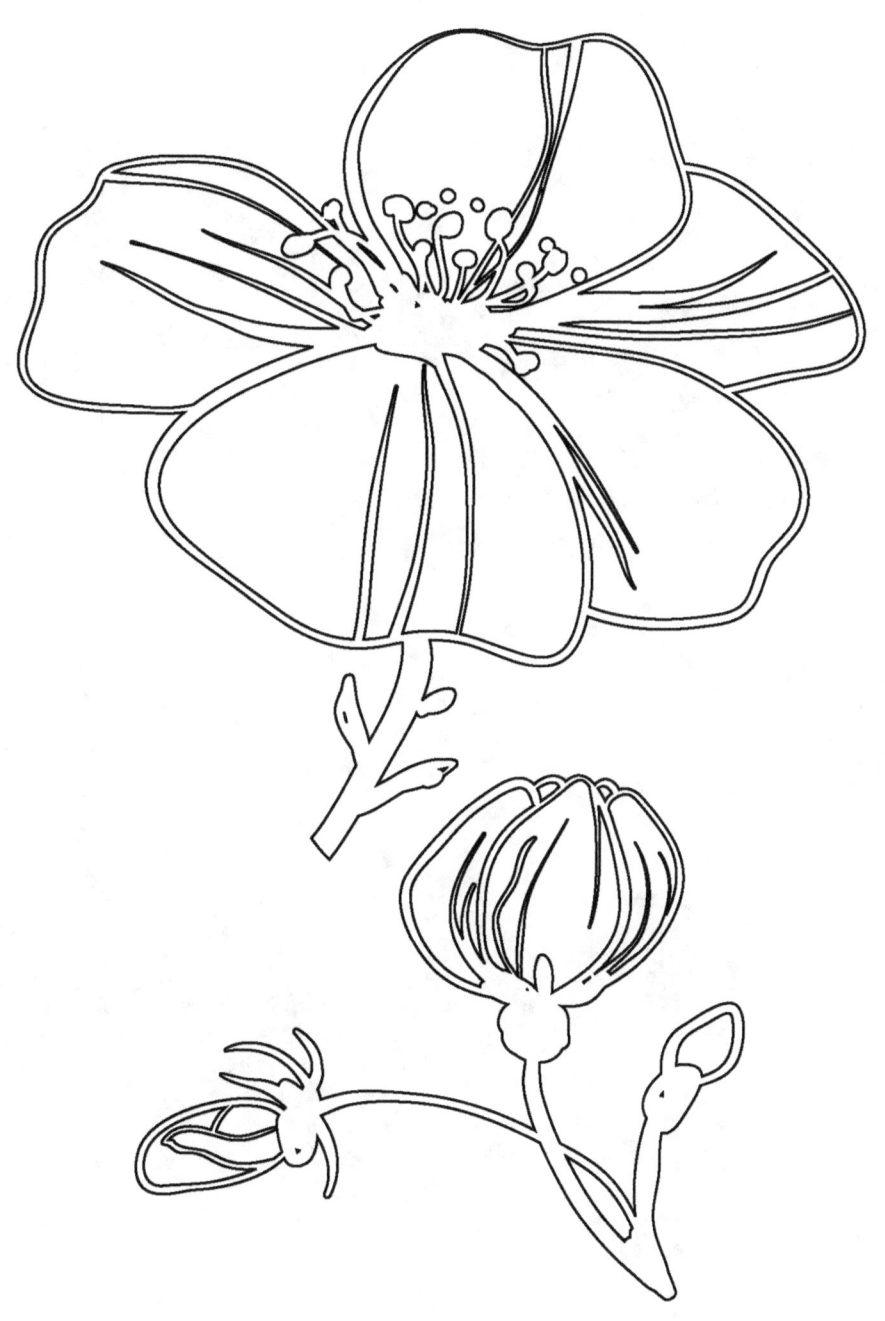

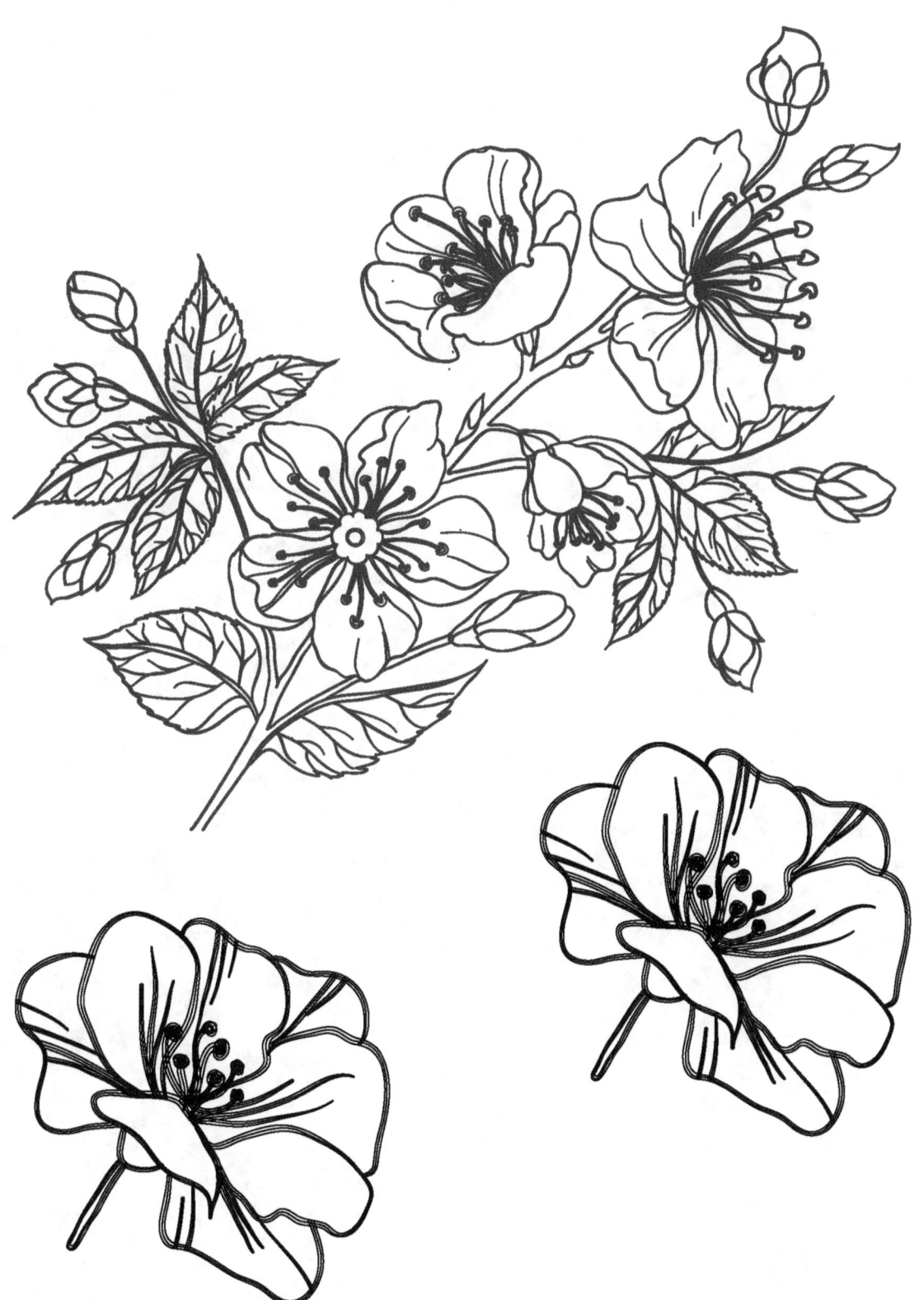

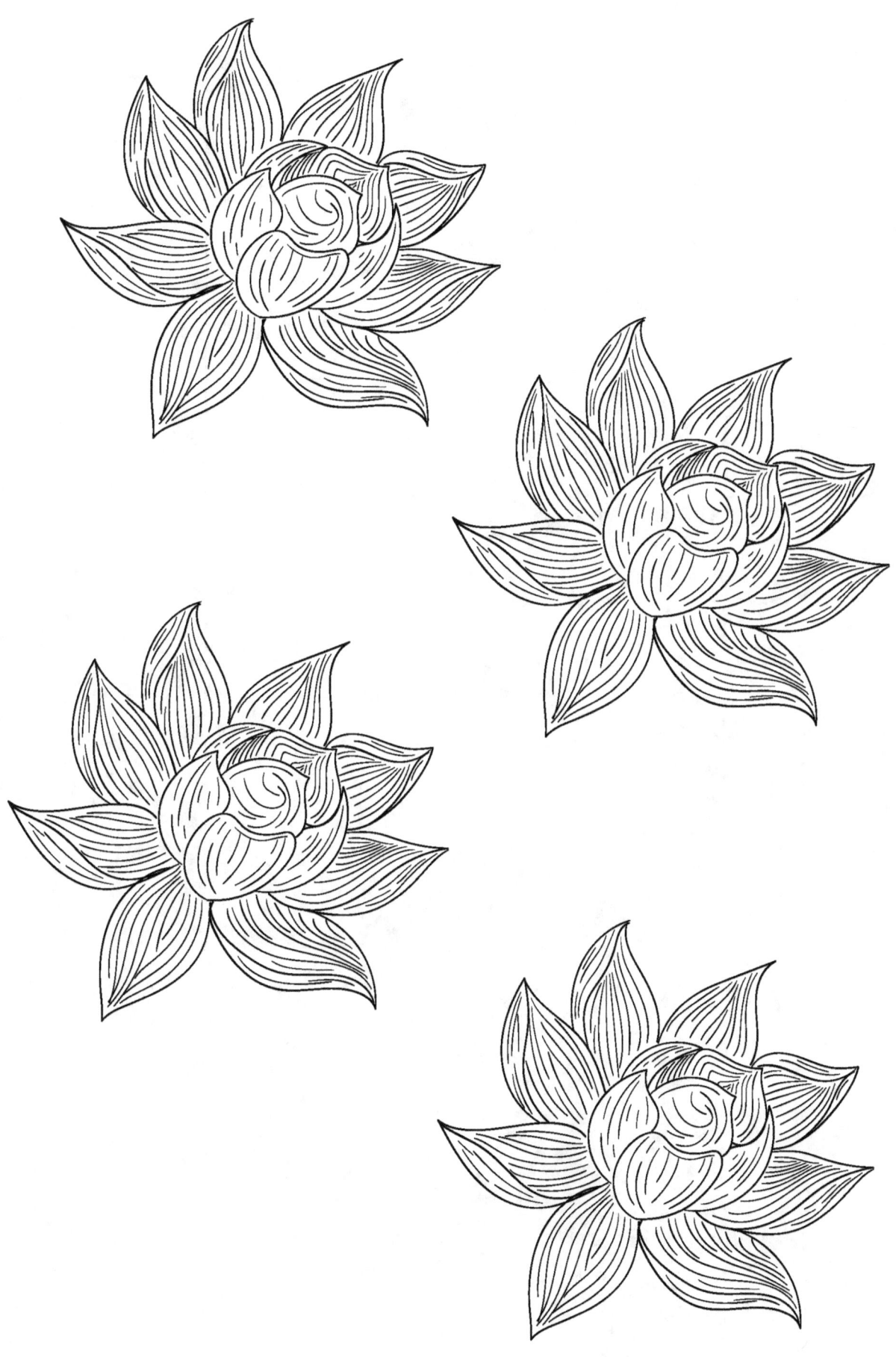

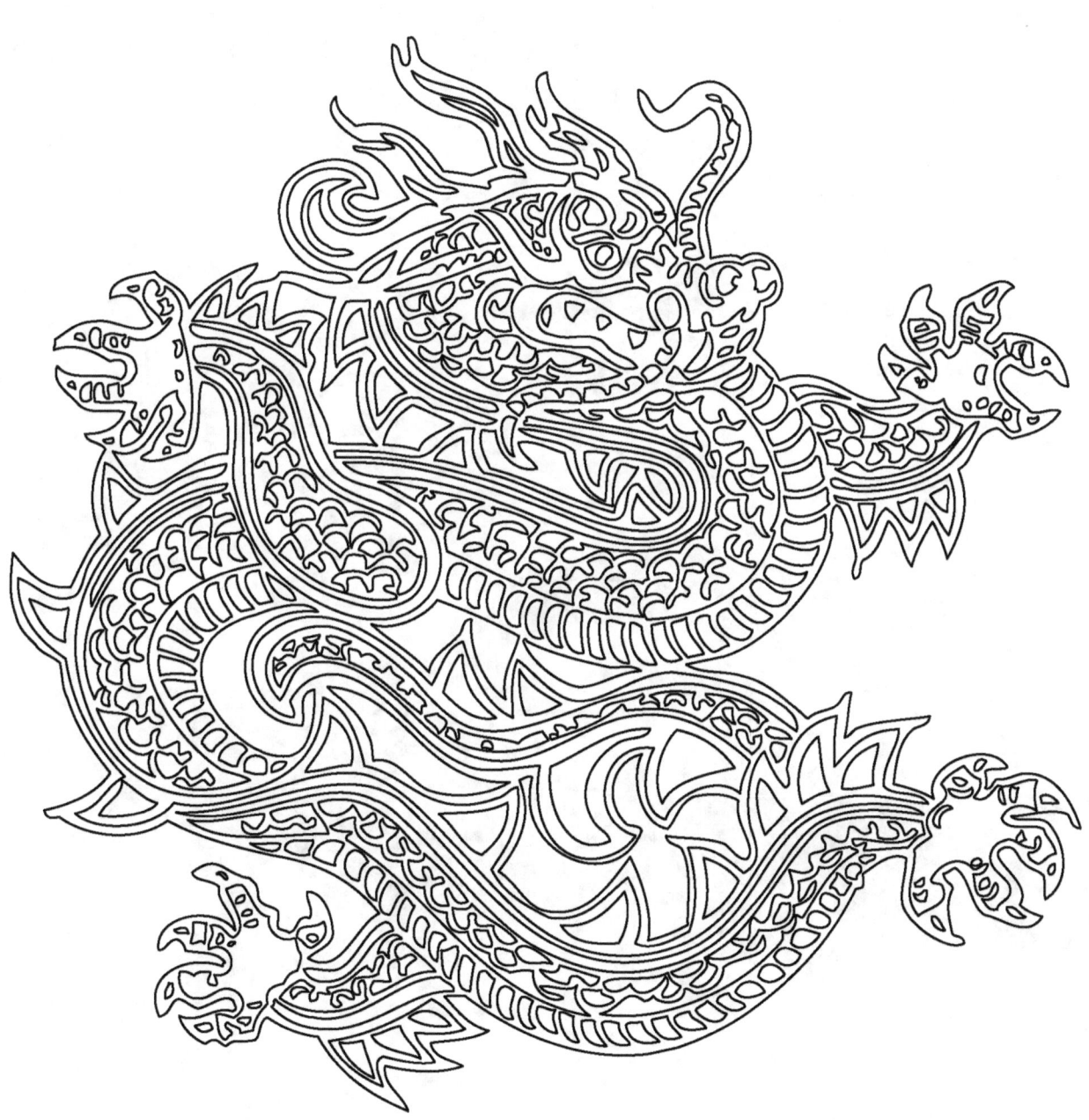

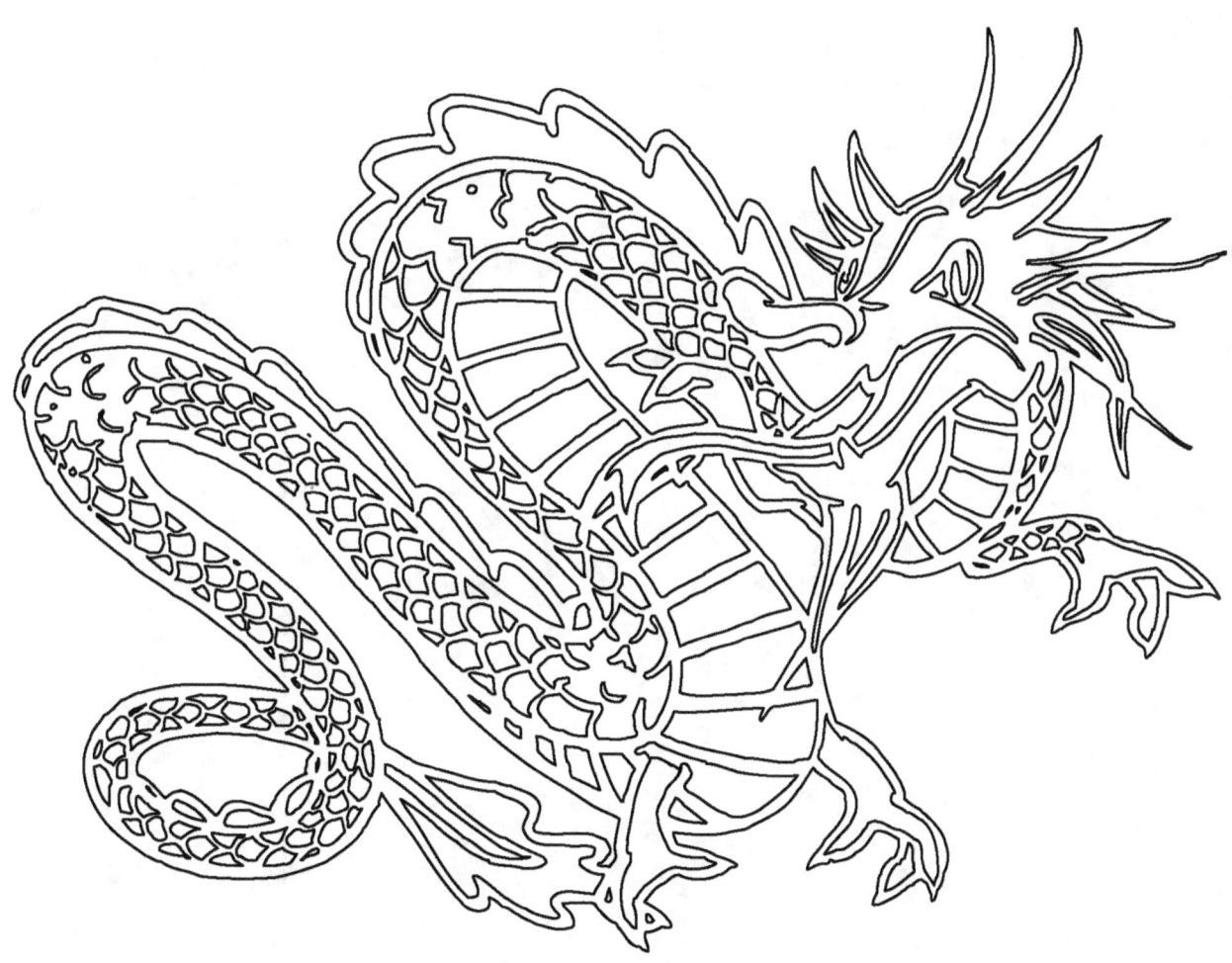

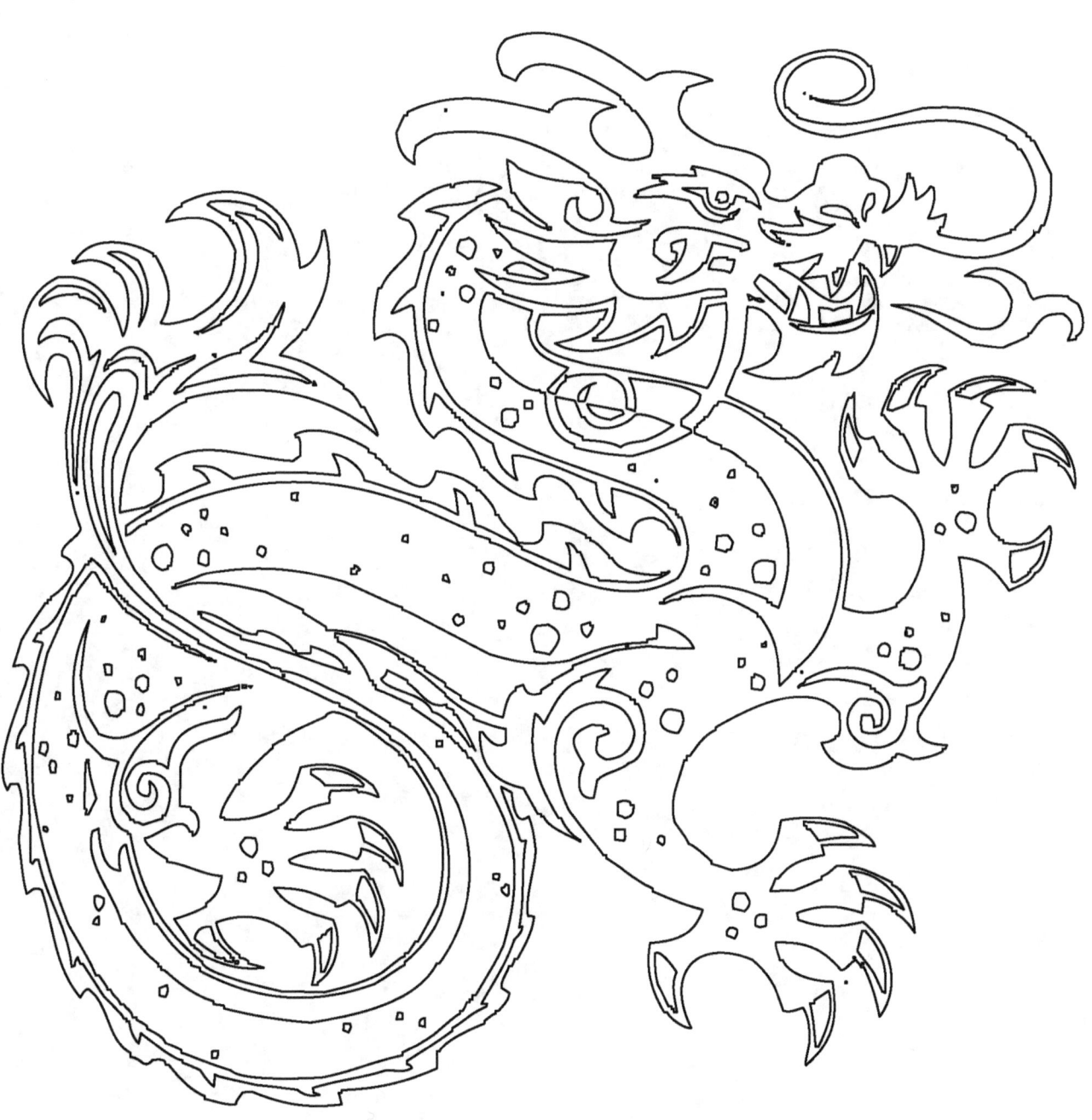

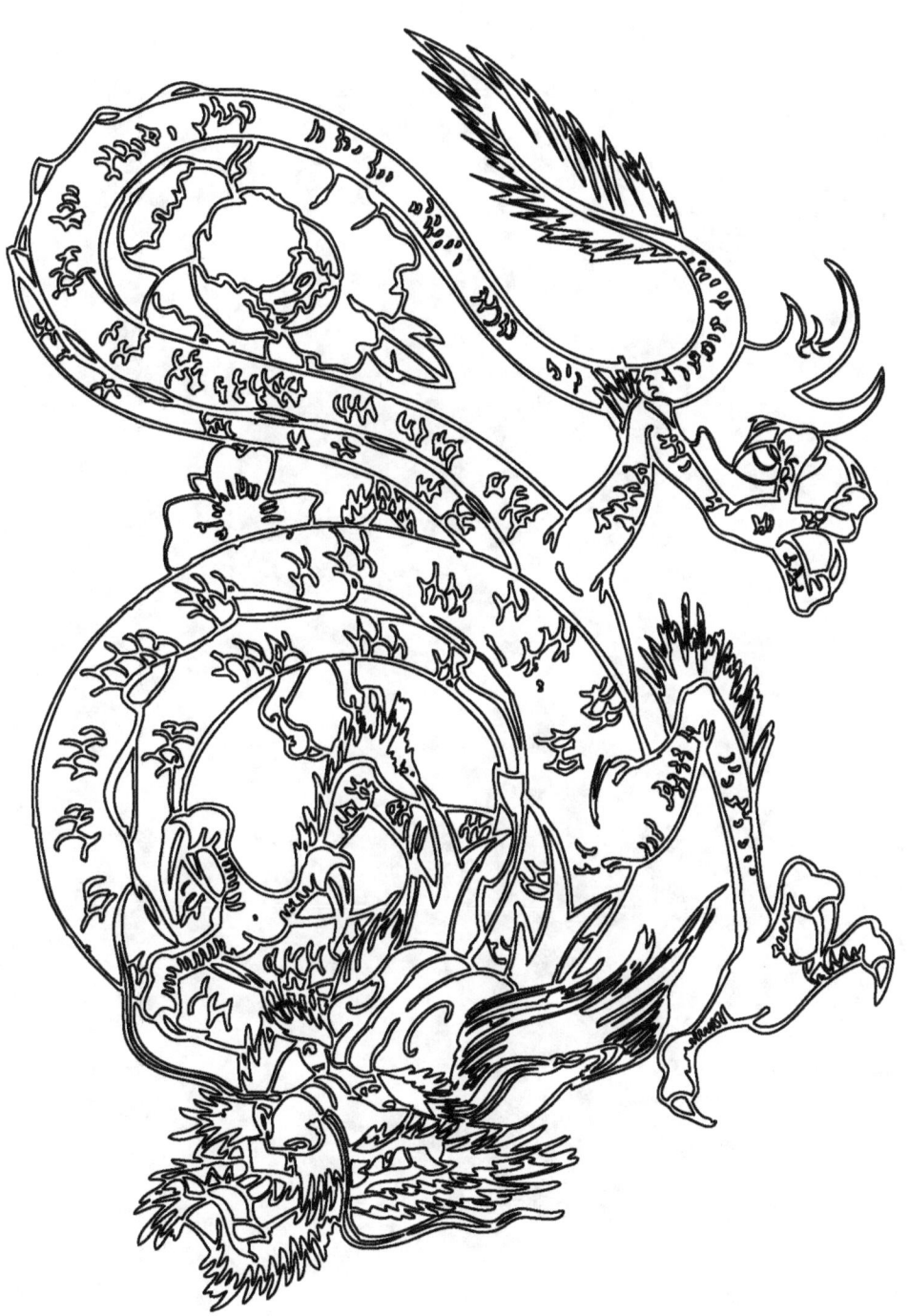

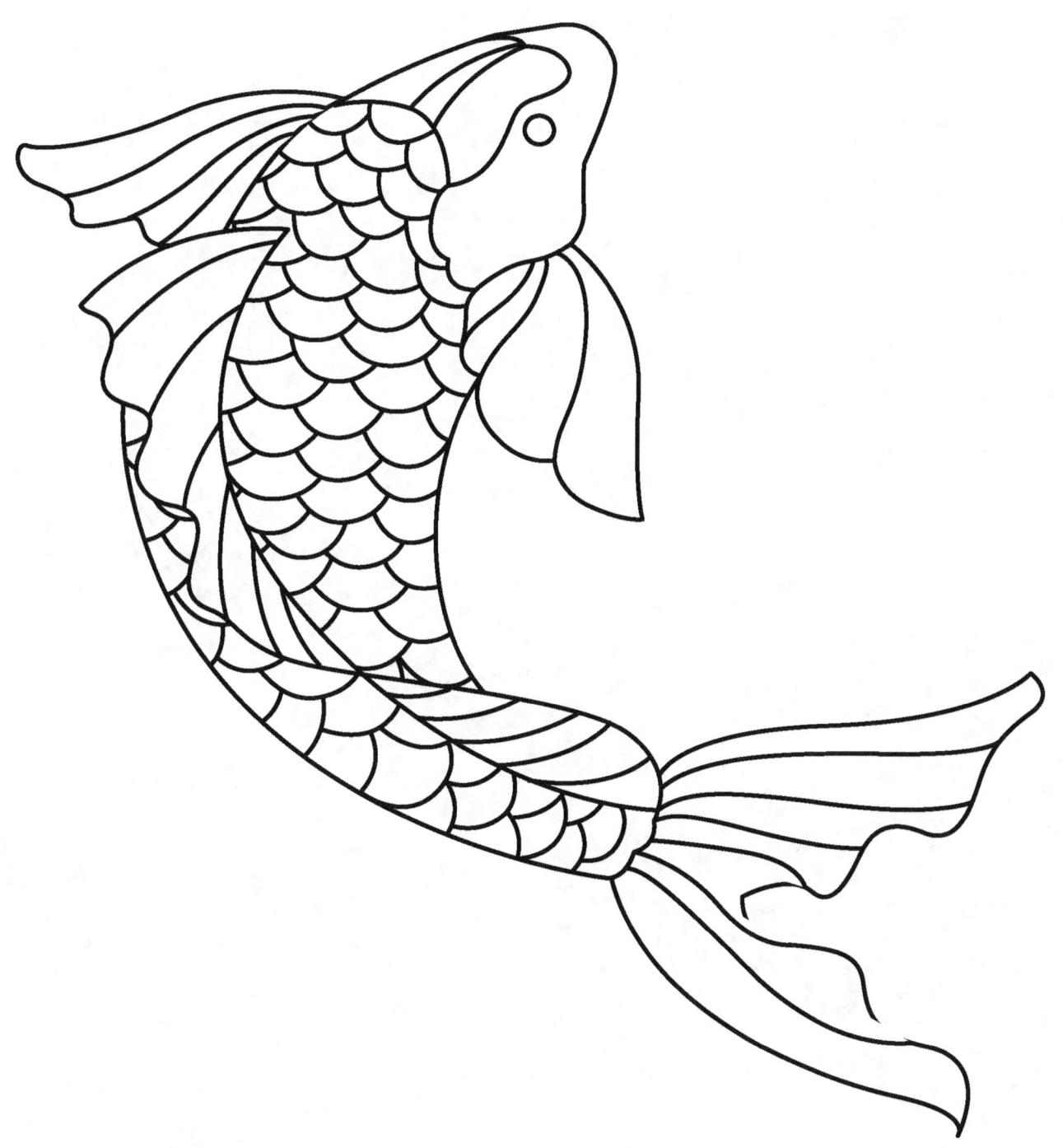

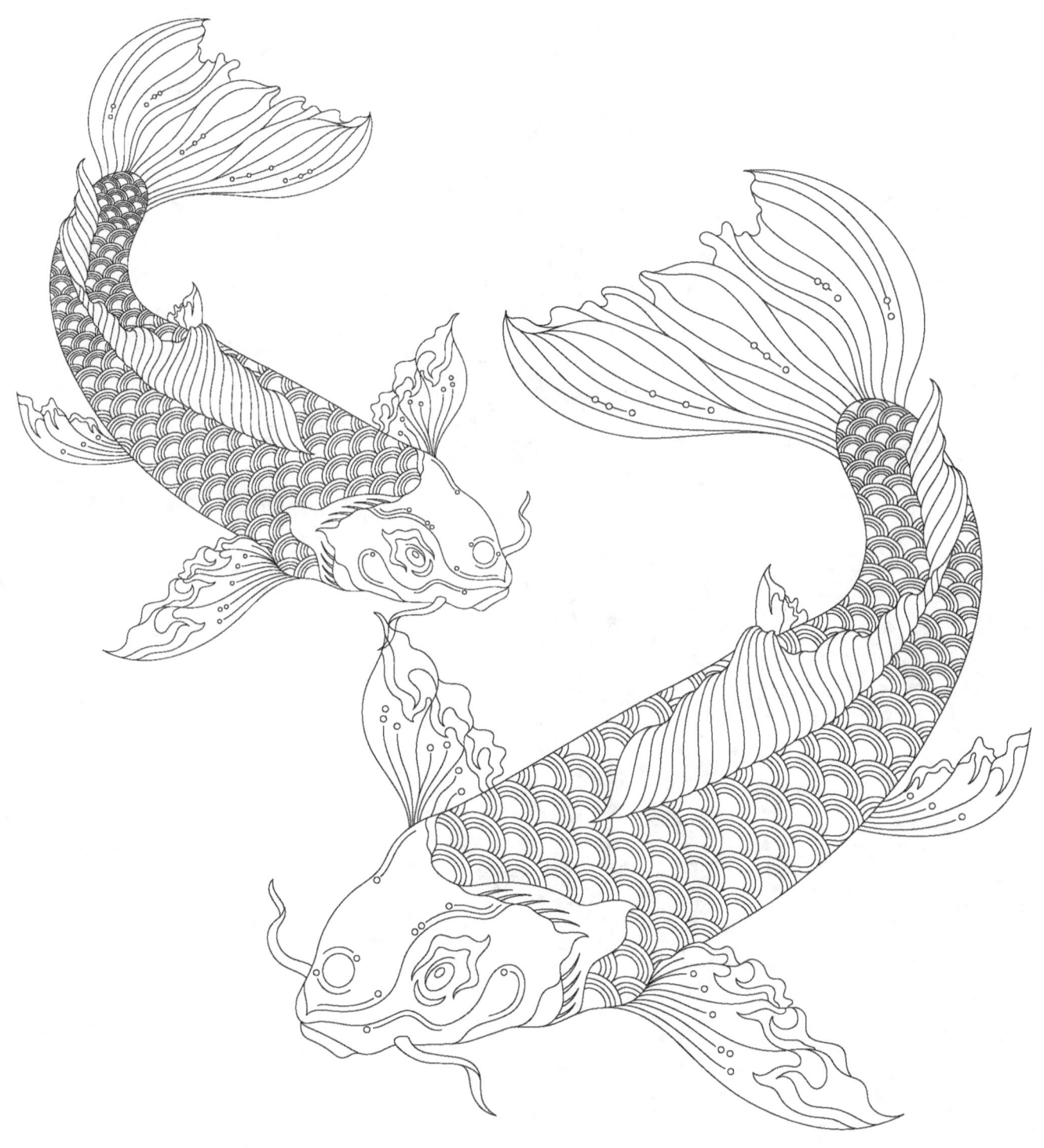

www.ingramcontent.com/pod-product-compliance
Lightning Source LLC
Chambersburg PA
CBHW081533220526
45467CB00010B/3164